Janet and Coli[...] [...]s on Britain's
mysterious her[...]
Sites in Britain,
and *Modern Mysteries of Britain*

From their h[...] ru[...]
rural Britain, prehistor[...] and stra[...]

JANET AND COLIN BORD

Mysterious Britain

Ancient Secrets of Britain and Ireland

Thorsons

An Imprint of HarperCollins*Publishers*

Thorsons
An Imprint of HarperCollins*Publishers*
77–85 Fulham Palace Road,
Hammersmith, London W6 8JB
1160 Battery Street,
San Francisco, California 94111–1213

First published in Great Britain by The Garnstone Press Ltd 1972
Published by Thorsons 1995
1 3 5 7 9 10 8 6 4 2

© The Garnstone Press Ltd 1972

Janet and Colin Bord assert the moral right
to be identified as the authors of this work

A catalogue record for this book
is available from the British Library

ISBN 1 85538 461 2

Printed in Great Britain by
Woolnough Bookbinding Limited
Irthlingborough, Northamptonshire

I am told that there are people who do not care
for maps, and find it hard to believe. The names,
the shapes of the woodlands, the courses of the
roads and rivers, the pre-historic footsteps of man
still distinctly traceable up hill and down dale, the
mills and the ruins, the ponds and the ferries,
perhaps the *Standing Stone* or the *Druidic Circle*
on the heath; here is an inexhaustible fund of
interest for any man with eyes to see, or tuppence
worth of imagination to understand with.

R. L. Stevenson: Note concerning *Treasure Island*

Contents

Janet Bord

J. Allan Cash

Introduction

*'It is, however, an Englishman's peculiarity
that possessing perhaps the most interesting history,
and some of the most fascinating relics
in the world, he is either too modest or too dull
to take account of them.'*

What author and antiquarian Harold Bayley wrote in 1919 is still oddly true today, and although the British are now taking a far greater interest in their historical heritage, there is much which still goes unnoticed, untouched by the clean-sweeping broom of officialdom, unseen by most local passers-by and unknown to visitors. These are the real 'fascinating relics' Mr Bayley refers to, and this book cannot, alas, present more than a mere sample of them. However, we hope that what is described and illustrated in this book will give some indication of what remains to be discovered by anyone who is interested.

The folklore and theories we present stress the point that there is far more to our prehistory than appears on the ground or in history books, and, further, that we all have much to learn from our ancestors and their way of life. Two things are clear: their life was different from ours and should not be interpreted on a twentieth century basis; and they were *not* savages. Scientific archaeology has until very recently made three assumptions that have been instrumental in giving a view of our past which is open to question. The first is that 'civilization' can only exist where there is a high level of applied technology, such as we have at present. The second, which grows out of the first, is that the earlier the remains the more primitive the people who left them. And the third is that war has been the great stimulator of civilizations. These views are derived from the myopic attitude bequeathed to us by the last century, and we feel that they need not be accepted unquestionably. We can perhaps take comfort in Harold Bayley's observation that 'what Authority maintains to-day it generally contradicts tomorrow'.

There is an increasing awareness that the people living in the Bronze and Neolithic Ages were not isolated groups unaware of each other's existence. The books of Marcel F. Homet (*Sons of the Sun* and *On the Trail of the Sun Gods*, Neville Spearman) and Constance Irwin (*Fair Gods and Stone Faces*, W. H. Allen) examine many clues suggesting that the cultures of these Ages had spread their contacts over a large

ix

part of the earth and that there was a vigorous exchange of ideas.

Archaeology is a youthful science. It is now a hundred years since Schliemann first dug at Hissarlik to uncover the site of ancient Troy and, though methods have since been greatly refined and modern scientific tools are now used, it is perhaps time that a broader perspective is adopted by professional archaeologists, and other factors in our history taken into serious account. Everything from folklore to the geographic relationship of sites with each other across the country should be considered as important and worthy of study. Schliemann's methods appear crude when compared with present-day digging techniques; and our traditional method of confining ourselves entirely to whatever was buried in the past will appear even more blinkered in a future in which the unearthing of broken pots and buried stones will be but one activity within a wide range of approaches. In *Mysterious Britain* we show that the sciences of both modern and ancient worlds have revealed hitherto unsuspected properties in ancient sites, and it may be that such seemingly diverse studies as UFOs and morris dancing may lead to the elucidation of some of the enigmas of prehistory.

England, Wales, Scotland and Ireland are all included in this book, with political divisions being ignored. The prehistory of these four countries, together with their surrounding islands, interacts strongly and in fascinating ways. Where a site still stands and can be visited, the Ordnance Survey One Inch map reference is given; where the exact location of a site is not known, the reference is for the nearest town or village, and 'approx.' appears in brackets after the reference. We have also indicated the sheet number of the relevant map.

England, Scotland, Wales and the surrounding islands are covered by Ordnance Survey 1 inch to 1 mile maps, and so is Northern Ireland. For Eire, only the $\frac{1}{2}$ inch to 1 mile scale map is available, but the procedure for finding the sites is exactly the same.

Certain places have a 'feel' about them; one remembers them for ever, the folk memory having been awakened for a moment. Some of them we put fences around and car parks nearby; others we keep for ourselves. Britain is uniquely rich in mysteries and mysterious places; we hope our book will arouse an awareness of them, and perhaps suggest a few possible answers.

Janet and Colin Bord

The Standing Stones and Circles of Prehistory

'*History cannot tell us [who erected the standing stones], for its records do not reach beyond the dawn of our civilization. But before that dawn there was the twilight of another civilization. History may ignore it; folk-lore may move in circles; nevertheless the vestiges remain. Great stones on the uplands and green ways winding across the chalk bear witness to the works of an ancient people long since fallen on sleep.*'

Dion Fortune in *Avalon of the Heart*

No one who has stood within the towering mass of Stonehenge can be unimpressed by the magnitude and skill of its construction. For over forty centuries the great grey stones have dominated Salisbury Plain, and their unfathomable power and magic continue to draw thousands each year to gaze and wonder. Although perhaps the culmination of stone circle construction with its magnificent trilithons, Stonehenge is not the only circle bequeathed to us from the enigmatic New Stone Age, if indeed it does come from this time. There are, throughout Britain, particularly in the more deserted western areas, many hundreds of stone circles ranging from those of a dozen feet in diameter to those of hundreds of feet. Very few of them have received attention from archaeologists, and most are scarcely known outside their own areas.

One scientist has in recent years brought a new approach and new technique to the study of these circles. Professor Alexander Thom has examined some 600 sites and made a detailed survey of 300 of them, and the results he has produced throw a completely new light on these constructions and the people who built them. As G. S. Hawkins found at Stonehenge, the circles provide an extremely accurate means of calculating the movements of the Sun, Moon and major stars during the year. In order to be used in this way, the stones had to be set out with a high degree of accuracy, and Professor Thom has found that the people who constructed the circles had a knowledge of mathematics that was only equalled a thousand years later in classical Greece. Although generally termed 'circles', very few of them are in fact so. They are constructed of rather more subtle geometric shapes than that, and when plotted on to paper can be seen to be flattened circles and ellipses.

Other researchers have made new and fascinating discoveries relating to these stone circles. In some areas they have been found to be spaced across the countryside at regular distances from each other, distances divisible by a unit known as a Megalithic Yard, which equals 2.72 feet. (For more information on this unit see Professor A. Thom's *Megalithic Sites in Britain* and pp. 132–3 of John Michell's *The View over Atlantis*.) Professor Thom noted that certain stones within a circle aligned with others outside it and with features on the horizon, and people whose particular interest has been the plotting of leys have shown that these alignments extend beyond these visible points to other sites of antiquity in other parts of the country; they are, in fact, part of the ley system. (For more information on leys, see 'Trackways and leys – the unseen power' – Section 9 in this book.)

Researchers whose interest is the complex geometric laws by which such Neolithic temples as Stonehenge and Avebury were constructed, have found that these very same principles were used some three thousand years later in the construction of the great abbeys and cathedrals of Britain and Europe (see 'The sanctity of ancient sites'). These geometric/cosmic principles were the real ageless secrets of the Masonic guilds, and by their application the architects were able to construct such edifices that, when activated by a congregation whose thought levels were sufficiently elevated, a fusion of the energies of the solar system with those of earth was caused, thereby creating a powerful life force which would enrich every individual and the surrounding land.

From these centres of power there stretched across the land leys or alignments of single standing stones, circles, dolmens, cairns, earthen mounds and other ancient sites, each with its particular function in the overall scheme of energy transmission. That the system has long fallen into disuse and the land and people have suffered accordingly there is no doubt, but like any great system based on natural principles, faint glimmerings of its original function occasionally activate some of the stones. When the archaeologist and psychic researcher T. C. Lethbridge attempted to find the date of the construction of the Merry Maidens stone circle near Lamorna in Cornwall, he took his dowsing pendulum in one hand and placed the other upon one of the stones. Immediately he received a strong tingling sensation like an electric shock, while his pendulum gyrated in a nearly horizontal position, and the huge, heavy stone felt as if it were rocking wildly. Many people have received sensations of shock when placing their hands on certain stones, and photographs have occasionally shown inexplicable light radiations emanating from the stones.

Another avenue of research that has made available further knowledge concerning the origin of the enigmatic stones is that of psychometry. This ability can be used, by those who are sufficiently sensitive, to tune into the vibrations retained in an ancient site or an object. From this they are sometimes able to pick up feelings, ideas and images related directly to the history involved in the situation. These psychic emanations surround us all the time. Those people whose awareness is developed to a certain pitch, either by training or by chance and heredity, are continually aware of the psychic climate of their environment.

The majority of people who have no knowledge of such matters, or may even retain a strong scepticism, are none the less receiving these psychic signals, albeit on a subconscious level. They, too, are attracted to these old stones, and such ancient structures as Stonehenge and Avebury hold a continual fascination, as testified by the thousands of visitors which they receive each year. To find out why, should be the subject of serious research.

Stonehenge, Wiltshire   SU 122422 (167)

The best-known prehistoric monument in Britain is associated in many people's minds with Druids, but Stonehenge is probably older than Druidism (though this itself is a vague name for a teaching that has existed for untold millennia). Standing in bleak isolation on Salisbury Plain, this impressive stone circle can be seen from miles away, although it is now in a ruinous condition, due to the depredations of man and weather.

The first construction is thought by some authorities to have taken place about 2600 B.C.; this was the outer ditch and bank and the circle of holes known as the Aubrey Holes and named after the seventeenth century antiquary who first found them. About 2000 B.C. an avenue of earth banks two miles long was made from the circle to the River Avon, and sixty bluestones (bluestone meant holy stone in the west of England) each of 4 tons were brought from the Prescelly Mountains in South Wales and erected in a double circle. Two hundred years later, the sarsen blocks that are the well-known feature today, weighing up to 50 tons and up to 21 feet in height, were erected. Brought from twenty miles away in north Wiltshire, eighty of these were carefully shaped with tenons on top of the vertical stones (see photograph) and mortices to receive them on the underside of the horizontal slabs. These slabs were also curved on their outer face to make a clean circular shape, and were fitted end to end with tongue and groove joints. The huge blocks high above their heads caused the Saxons to name the structure 'hanging stones', from which the present 'Stonehenge' is thought to be derived.

Recently some modern techniques have been used to delve into the mystery of this enigmatic monument. Professor G. S. Hawkins has used a computer to examine the immense number of alignments that the Sun and Moon, rising and setting at different times of the year, make with the various stones and spaces between the trilithons, and he has found that Stonehenge can be used as an accurate predictor of the movements of the heavenly bodies and to foretell eclipses. This can hardly be accidental, though it is unlikely to be the full story. Other researchers have used more esoteric means than computer technology, such as John Michell who has applied gematria (the ancient science in which each letter in the alphabet has a corresponding number, forming a link between literature and mathematics). He shows that Stonehenge was primarily a Solar temple and was laid upon the same geometrical plan as Glastonbury Abbey was at a later date.

Some baffling questions are raised by the double circle of sixty bluestones which form part of the structure. It is certain that they are not natural to this locality as are the huge sarsens that form the trilithons and outer circle. The nearest natural source has been located in the Prescelly Mountains in South Wales, and they are found also in North Wales and parts of Ireland. One possibility that has been mooted at intervals over the years is that they are erratics carried by Ice Age glaciers from their natural site and deposited on Salisbury Plain, but as no other deposits are known to have been found, this theory does not find much favour.

4

A possibility held more generally by archaeologists is that the bluestones were transported by sea and then along rivers to within a few miles of Salisbury Plain. The official guide to Stonehenge has a drawing showing a group of hairy little men clustered round a large stone that almost covers the deck of a flimsy raft which carries an upright spar with a tattered sail lashed to it. This conception is probably far from the truth. People who have a knowledge of the coasts of southern Britain maintain that a high level of seamanship would be necessary to navigate such a heavy load, whether the route was up the Bristol Channel or round Land's End and along the south coast to the River Avon. T. C. Lethbridge, who was both an archaeologist and a sailor, thought sea transportation was possible, but believed that two boats with the stone slung in the water between them was a more feasible idea. (See his book *The Legend of the Sons of God*.) He also thought that a sea passage from the deposits of bluestones in Ireland was more likely to be successful. As we will see later, some legends support the idea that the stones came from Ireland. Once on land, they are thought to have been dragged along either on a sled or on rollers.

But why did the builders want these particular stones? There were plenty of good big stones in the locality, and some of these *were* used for the main structure. Although called 'bluestones', those brought from Prescelly or even farther are not particularly decorative. They have a bluish tint only when freshly fractured, and this soon fades with weathering. What qualities, what properties, made them so attractive, perhaps so necessary, to the builders of Stonehenge? To say, as some do, that they were venerated for religious or ritual reasons, explains nothing. It is tantamount to saying we don't know. If, as has been suggested in the introduction to this section, the stone circles were part of a worldwide system for subtle energy transmissions, then Stonehenge, as a powerful generator in that system, perhaps required these particular stones in order to function. As we have seen, the disciplines of astronomy and mathematics have been applied to the mysteries of Stonehenge and have provided a wider understanding of its construction. Perhaps it is time to take another step, and for chemists and physicists to investigate the crystal and electrostatic properties of the bluestones and the sarsens.

Another problem, apart from that of the transportation of the bluestones, is the question of the raising of the great lintels on to the sarsen blocks. Traditional archaeology favours man muscle as the motive power. The official handbook has diagrams of the blocks being raised up on platforms of criss-crossed logs. Other ideas that have been put forward are ramps of earth all round the uprights to support them while the top stone was slid into position, the earth then being removed, but this idea is not supported by excavations, which reveal no evidence of such ramps. It has also been suggested that the operation was performed in the winter, but instead of earth, packed snow was used to make a ramp up which the stone could be slid. Icy conditions could also assist in transporting the stones across country.

Megalithic constructions are to be found all over the globe. The huge statues on Easter Island are well known, and on an island that is bare of trees

the theory of log rollers is untenable. The natives of the island explain the moving and erection of the statues by stating that the chiefs used mana, or mental power. This power is akin to telekinesis, and was known and used in past centuries by the Huna priesthood in the Pacific islands. Modern scientific research into ESP is revealing that the human mind has amazing hidden abilities, and telekinesis (the ability to move objects at a distance by thought power alone), which has been shown beyond doubt to exist, could in the past have been a widely known and used method of transportation. A culture which may have generated and directed the natural life-giving currents of the earth may possibly have developed mental powers which could nullify gravity and manipulate huge masses of stone. The most advanced researchers into paraphysics are now making the first tentative steps into the rediscovery of the powers of the mind, and as these abilities become known and accepted they will inevitably influence the trends of speculation which are directed to the mysteries left by the men of old, some of which are described in this book.

Legend has something to tell us about Stonehenge, and today such stories are not dismissed as casually as they once were, for there are often grains of truth in seemingly fantastic accounts. Of Stonehenge we learn from Geoffrey of Monmouth, the twelfth century chronicler, that Merlin the magician by his secret art moved stones from Ireland to 'the mount of Ambrius', which has been identified as Amesbury, very near Stonehenge, and earlier the stones were brought from Africa to Ireland by 'giants who were magicians'. Legend and folklore from many parts of the world have accounts of stones being lifted by the use of sound vibrations, produced by musical instruments, cymbals or the human voice, and of them flying through the air. In view of current research into sonics, it is to many no less believable that the ancients had practical knowledge of such matters than is the supposition of archaeologists that such edifices as the great pyramids and Stonehenge were built by gangs of sweating barbarians using rope and roller.

Stonehenge
'restored'

The Lion Gate at Mycenae

This picture of the magnificent Lion Gate at Mycenae,
southern Greece, is shown as a comparison with the
structures of Stonehenge. The great lintel across the
doorway is 16 feet long and the whole structure was erected
with blocks of hewn stone so massive that they caused the
ancient Greeks to term these ruins cyclopean, after the
Cyclopes, a race of one-eyed giants. This gateway has been
dated at 1500 B.C.; about a hundred years later Mycenae was
mysteriously destroyed by fire, and the whole site was
abandoned and never rebuilt.

This structure is approximately contemporary with the
erection of the great trilithons at Stonehenge, and must have
presented some of the same technical problems. Did the
men who built Stonehenge influence the building of
Mycenae? Or was Stonehenge built by the travelling masons
from Mycenae? On one of the sarsen blocks at Stonehenge
the carving of a dagger has been discerned, and daggers of
this shape are known to have been used in Mycenaean
Greece circa 1600 B.C.

Abor Low, near Middleton, Derbyshire SK 160636 (111)

This impressive henge monument is over a thousand feet up on the Derbyshire moors. All the stones except one, and there are about fifty of them, are recumbent, and may never have stood upright. The stones are of limestone which has weathered over the ages, the longest being 14 feet. The largest originally weighed nearly 10 tons. Close by are burial mounds, and one of them is part of the outer bank of the earthwork. This site seems to be particularly significant, for it is said that fifty leys pass through it. (For more information on leys, see 'Trackways and leys – the unseen power'.) From the air, this monument looks like a huge clockface.

The Blind Fiddler, near
Catchall, Cornwall
SW 425282 (189)

This impressive stone, 10 feet
9 inches tall, is in an area of
Cornwall 'peopled' by single
standing stones given the
names of musicians. The
Blind Fiddler was turned to
stone for making music on the
Sabbath, and a similar legend
is told of other stones not far
away. Such legends may have
originated when Christianity
was gradually defeating
paganism, and the devout
Christians used such stories in
order to influence those who
had not yet adopted the new
religion; or perhaps they may
only date from Puritan times,
when singing and dancing
were much frowned upon.

Janet Bord

Dwarfie Stane, Island of Hoy, Orkneys   HY 243005 (7)

Approximately 28 feet long, 14 feet wide and 8 feet high,
this large block of sandstone is generally thought to have
been a rock-cut tomb, and as such is unique in the British
Isles. However, some eighteenth and nineteenth century
antiquaries had different views, and the following quotation
from *The Celtic Druids* by G. Higgins gives information on
the stone from Mr Toland and Dr Wallace. 'It is hollowed
out within, and at each end is a bed and pillow worked out
in the stone, each capable of holding two persons. At the top,
about the middle, is a round hole to admit light and let the
smoke escape. It has a hole at the side about two feet square
to admit its inhabitants; and a square stone lies near it,
which seems to have served the purpose of a door.' They
further compared it with a stone near the entry of the
temple of Minerva at Sais in Egypt, and felt that both stones
may have been used for religious purposes.

The Cheesewring, Bodmin Moor, Cornwall   SX 258724 (186)

This weird pile of rocks, allegedly of natural formation and weathering, was believed to be the dwelling place of a druid who had a cup of gold. This cup, whose contents were inexhaustible (symbolizing the cup of knowledge?), was always offered to thirsty hunters passing by, and one of them decided to drink the cup dry. But he failed to do so, and in a rage he rode off with the cup, whereupon his horse fell over the rocks and the hunter was killed. The cup was buried with him.

This may sound like just another legend, but on this occasion amazing confirmation was received when in 1818 a nearby cairn called King Arthur's Grave was opened and a gold cup, dated to around 1500 B.C., was found among other goods. Another tradition tells of a golden boat discovered in a cairn near the Cheesewring. The top stone of the Cheesewring is said to turn round when it hears the cock crow. Another stone close by is known as the Druid's Chair.

It is thought by some that such structures as the Cheesewring and Bowerman's Nose (illustrated elsewhere in this section) are the remains of vast interconnected power storage temples. The temples of Cornwall were dedicated to the well-being of the body, while those of Devon were for the revitalizing of the spirit.

sarsen stones at Lockeridge Dene, Wiltshire   SU 144673 (157)

Sarsen stones or 'grey wethers' (because they sometimes look like sheep) litter the downs between Marlborough and Avebury, and are thought to be what remains of the sandstone which once covered these chalk downs. Many of these stones were used to build monuments like Avebury and the stonework in the numerous long barrows, such as West Kennet, in the area.

sacred stones in India

Looking very much like a group of hooded figures gathered together at a place of assembly, these are in fact standing stones coloured with patches of vermilion. Britain is not the only place where stones have been venerated in past ages.

Chûn Quoit, near Penzance, Cornwall   SW 402339 (189)

Such arrangements of massive slabs of stone (called quoits or cromlechs or dolmens) are thought to be the remains of ancient burial chambers, and to have originally been covered by barrows of earth or cairns of stones. Remains of a circular mound are visible around this quoit, which stands high up on the moors close to the hillfort of Chûn Castle.

Janet Bord

Edna Knowles

stone circle near Penmaenmawr, Caernarvonshire   SH 723746 (107)

There are hundreds of stone circles throughout the British
Isles to which archaeologists have paid scant attention. Such
sites may provide little or nothing for the 'digging'
archaeologist, but there is a growing body of researchers who
prefer to approach these remnants of a past culture from a
mathematical, geometrical and astronomical viewpoint.

Avebury, Wiltshire   SU 102700 (157)

The ancient stones watch silently in the still light of the early morning; this is one of the best times to visit Avebury and absorb the magic wisdom of this temple, so very different from the grim gloom of Stonehenge. This picture was taken from the outer bank looking across to the southern entrance of the Kennet Avenue.

Although the first Christian church was built just outside the earth bank in A.D. 634, the older beliefs continued to attract many, and in the early fourteenth century the Church authorities took drastic action. Part of the bank near the church was thrown into the ditch and levelled, and some of the stones were overthrown and buried, thereby preserving them until they were found and re-erected in this century. The old stones claimed at least one victim of this desecration. Recent excavations revealed the skeleton of a barber surgeon, killed by the unexpected toppling of a large monolith that he was helping to bury.

17

Avebury, Stone Age powerhouse?

'Avebury doth as much exceed
Stonehenge in grandeur as a
Cathedral doth an ordinary
Parish Church.'

John Aubrey 1626–97

Older even than Stonehenge, Avebury lies on the downs near Marlborough, silent in the early morning mist. Now little of the original grandeur remains, most of the stones having been smashed to pieces in the seventeenth and eighteenth centuries and used to build the village of Avebury and neighbouring farms. At its height Avebury was a spiritual powerhouse. Now the ruins of this great Sun temple are in the care of the Department of the Environment, as the carefully trimmed grass and concrete posts, marking the positions of missing stones, testify. Surrounding the whole area is a great earth bank 1,300 feet in diameter, with an inner ditch 30 feet deep. From the bottom of the ditch to the top of the bank is 55 feet. Within this is the outer circle of stones, local unquarried sarsens weighing up to 40 tons. Originally there were one hundred, but now the number is reduced to twenty-seven. Within this circle of stones there are the remnants of two smaller circles, each originally of about thirty stones. Now there are only a few stray monoliths in the fields and cottage gardens of the village of Avebury, which itself is largely within the boundaries of the great circular earthwork.

Dr William Stukeley was one of the first antiquaries to visit and document Avebury, in the early eighteenth century, and for thirty years he was a helpless observer as the local farmers and builders periodically toppled and smashed the great stones to clear the land for the plough and to obtain an easy source of building material. While this continued, Stukeley made careful drawings and measurements and sought to elucidate the mysteries locked within the stones. A man of great scholarship, he had studied the philosophies of the ancients, and brought a knowledge of Egyptian, Hebrew and Greek teachings to bear on the problem.

He was the first to appreciate that from the great circle there extended two avenues of stones, 50 feet wide and each a mile and a half long. One reaches out south-east and terminates in another stone circle of 130 feet diameter, known as The Sanctuary, on top of Overton Hill. The other, which made a sinuous double curve towards the south-west, no longer exists, having been destroyed shortly after Stukeley had made his drawings of it. These avenues he recognized as forming the Solar Serpent: the Sanctuary circle represented the head, and the Kennet and Beckhampton avenues formed the body, which passed through the Avebury circle – the Sun Symbol. These symbols of the solar disc and the serpent were used, often together, by ancient cultures in many parts of the world (for example, Egypt), to express the highest ideals, those of the supreme creative being and the wisdom of inner truths.

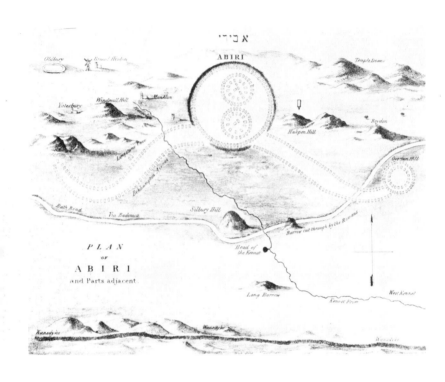

An early nineteenth century antiquary's plan of Avebury and its environs. Beckhampton Avenue, the tail end of the serpent, no longer exists, having been destroyed in the eighteenth century. The two stones named Longstone Cove are still in place and can be seen standing in a field just north of Beckhampton. The official guidebook for Avebury makes no mention of this avenue, all surface traces of it having been so effectively removed, and there appears to have been no attempt to find any evidence by excavation.

One of the longest and most impressive leys in the country cuts through the southern edge of the Avebury circle, according to John Michell. This ley or 'dragon line' stretches from Land's End to Burrow Mump and Glastonbury Tor, thence on to Avebury, and eventually reaches Bury St Edmunds, Suffolk, touching en route many hills and churches dedicated to St Michael. (For more information on the significance of St Michael, see 'Britain, land of legends', and for more on leys see 'Trackways and leys – the unseen power'.)

20

Colin Bord

This is the northern part of the Kennet Avenue looking towards Avebury, hidden in the mist. It illustrates one of the interesting features of these stones, which along the length of the row alternate between the wide, angular shapes and the thinner, straight ones. To discover whether the builders did this simply for the aesthetic effect or whether there is an esoteric principle of shape power involved, is at present beyond the wit of twentieth century man.

Originally there were 200 stones in the avenue, but far fewer remain today, only the northern part having been restored and preserved. At the other end lies the serpent's head, which was once a double circle of some 50 stones. During 1723 and 1724, a local farmer removed the lot and used them in his buildings in Beckhampton. For two centuries the site lay forgotten, until it was rediscovered by aerial photography and excavated in 1930. It lies on the southernmost promontory of Hackpen Hill, the significance being that 'hac' is a name for the serpent, and 'pen' means head.

This is possibly how Avebury looked some 5,000 years ago when it was first erected as a Sun temple. The surrounding ditch may have been filled with water, not as a barricade but to symbolize the site as a holy island, and to control and contain the energies that were drawn to this area. Was the later defensive moat a degenerate application of this idea? On the horizon is Oldbury earthwork, one of the ancient enclosures which has a white horse carved on the hillside below it.

> 'Thus, this stupendous fabric, which for
> some thousands of years has braved the
> continual assaults of the weather, and by
> the nature of it, when left to itself, like the
> pyramids of Egypt, would have lasted as
> long as the globe, has fallen a sacrifice
> to the wretched ignorance and avarice of a
> little village, unluckily placed within it.'
>
> William Stukeley

Mayburgh, Yanwath, Westmorland   NY 519285 (83)

A single stone 9 feet high stands at the centre of this
earthwork, which is encircled by banks around 10 feet high.
Four stones were to be seen in the nineteenth century, with
a further four at the entrance. Psychometrist Iris Campbell
had this to say about the site after her visit in 1944:

'*This site would seem to come in to a period approximately B.C.
15,000; it was more in the nature of an experimental area for the
trying out of the sun's rays at certain angles and conditions . . .
one is very conscious of its period of decline and eventual break-
up; what brought about this was due to a cleavage in the
community that functioned here. There were two kinds of magic
in force, one evil and one good; it was a truly concentric area
where the magnetism was induced from the four points of the
compass, forming with the circle the complete Celtic Cross. The
period covered by the Ministry was for 1,000 years during which
time an excess of magic of various kinds caused eventually its
break-up and downfall; it subsequently received too much
power and was broken up from within . . . .*'

Mên-an-Tol, near Morvah, Cornwall   SW 427349 (189)

There are other holed stones in Cornwall, but this one, also called the Crick Stone, is the best known. Many of these stones are supposed to be helpful in curing certain illnesses, and children were once passed through the Mên-an-Tol when they were suffering from rickets. Stones with holes big enough to crawl through, and with similar beliefs attached to them, can be found all over the world. There may once have been some benefit to be gained from such customs, for if, as is proposed elsewhere in this book, certain stones can hold powerful currents passing through the earth, could not the hole serve as a focus for this power, which would pass into the body of, and give renewed vitality to, anyone climbing through the hole?

Janet Bord
Northern Ireland Tourist Board

The Holestone, Doagh, Co. Antrim   J 242907

The hole in this stone is smaller, but still large enough for a hand. It is said that betrothals are confirmed by the couples clasping hands through this hole, which is surely evidence of ancient fertility rites.

The Bowl Rock, Trencrom Hill, near Lelant,
Cornwall   SW 521368 (189)

This huge granite boulder stands in a stream at the foot of
Trencrom Hill. It looks out of place, because there are no
other similar rocks to be seen in the valley, but the legend
attached to it tries to explain its presence there. The giants
who lived on Trencrom Hill liked to play a game of bowls
using giant rocks. The Bowl Rock is one that rolled to the
bottom of the hill and was never retrieved. (For more
information on Trencrom Hill, see 'Earthworks on the
hilltops'.)

Legananny Dolmen, Dromara, Co. Down   J 289434
(N.I. 1″ map 9; Eire ½″ map 9)

This group of stones is impressively situated 850 feet up in
the mountains. The capstone is over 10 feet long.

Scottish Tourist Board

Callanish standing stones, Isle of Lewis,
Outer Hebrides   NB 213331 (12)

This is truly one of the most mysterious sites in
Britain – and the most remote. Here on desolate
moorland stands a stone circle of thirteen tall
pillars, approached by an avenue of stones
270 feet long, of which only nine now remain
standing. Shorter 'arms' of stones branch off from
the circle, and the whole configuration is a cross,
as the plan shows. Within the circle is a chambered
cairn dating back to around 2000 B.C., close by
the entrance to which stands the tallest pillar,
15 feet 7 inches high.

There is a legend that a king, who was also a
priest, came to the island with ships bearing great
stones and black men to erect the stones. The
priest was accompanied by other priests, and they
all wore robes of bird skins and feathers. Another
story tells how St Kiaran, preaching Christianity
on the island, turned to stone the old giant
inhabitants who held an annual council at
Callanish. They had refused to build a Christian
church or in any way subscribe to the new faith.

Until recently, it was believed locally that when
the Sun rose on Midsummer morning, the
'Shining One' walked along the stone avenue, his
arrival heralded by the cuckoo's call. The cuckoo
is a bird of the blessed isles of Tir-nan-Og, the
Celtic paradise which was drowned by the sea.

Harold's Stones, Trelleck, Monmouthshire
SO 496052 (155)

The reason for the erection of these three stones, the tallest of which is over 12 feet, is not known, but the fact that they once carried, and sometimes still do carry, immense power was shown one day recently when two dowsers were flung back from one of the stones when they put their hands on it.

Stanton Drew, Somerset   ST 601634 (166)

'*No one, say the country people about Stantondrue, was ever able to reckon the number of these metamorphosed stones, or to take a draught of them, though several have attempted to do both, and proceeded till they were either struck dead upon the spot, or with such an illness as soon carried them off.*'

Wood's *Description of Bath*

A 'musical' legend attaches to the stones at Stanton Drew – three stone circles, two stone avenues, the Cove and a fallen standing stone, Hautville's Quoit. (See also The Blind Fiddler, illustrated elsewhere in this section.) There was a wedding one Saturday, and all the guests were dancing late into the night. At midnight, the fiddler stopped playing for them, saying he could not play on the Sabbath. But then a dark stranger appeared and continued the music, and the merry-makers danced faster and faster and could not stop. At dawn, the music ceased, and they saw that the fiddler was none other than the Devil. They could not run away from him, and he said that one day he would return and play to them again. Until that day comes, they stand, as still as stone, in a field at Stanton Drew.

Stones of Initiation

There are certain stones throughout the world that have a special significance; their history stretches back into the mists of legend and they are
used and venerated today, though few who do so could explain why.
Such a stone is the Stone of Scone, also known as the Coronation Stone
or the Stone of Destiny.

This rests on a shelf beneath the seat of the Coronation Chair in
Westminster Abbey, London, and since the thirteenth century every
British monarch (save only one, the first Mary) has sat over this stone
during the inauguration ceremony of the coronation. The Coronation
Chair is itself sufficiently ancient to be an object redolent with the history of Britain: it dates from 1296 and was made on the order of
Edward I when he had the stone brought from Scotland to London.
But no one knows for certain where this stone originated nor why it has
always had so much significance as a stone of inauguration. Traditionally it was the pillow used by Jacob when he had his dream of the
angels at Bethel. Later it was in the Temple of Jerusalem and the kings
of Judah were crowned upon it. Then in the fourth century B.C., the
daughter of the last king of Judah and the prophet Jeremiah travelled
through Egypt and Spain to Ireland, taking the stone with them. The
princess from Judah married into the royal line of the Irish kings, and
for centuries afterwards the kings of Ireland were crowned above the
stone.

Some versions say that it came to Scotland in A.D. 500, others say the
date was about A.D. 900, but it was at a time when the Picts were defeated and one of the royal house of Ireland was crowned king of a
united Scotland. The stone was kept at Scone where thirty-four succes-
sive Scottish kings were crowned sitting above it. In 1297 Edward I
took the stone to London and had it placed beneath his newly-made
Coronation Chair in Westminster Abbey. It remained there until 1950
when Scottish Nationalists removed it one night and took it into hiding
in Scotland. In 1951 it was recovered and restored to the Abbey.

Although the Stone of Scone may be unique in so far as it is still used
after so many centuries, there were at one time many such stones and

the locations of some are still known, although others have been forgotten or destroyed. One such was the Stone of the Kings, the inauguration stone of the O'Neills which stood in Tullaghoge, the capital of mediaeval Tyrone, which is now a deserted earthwork overgrown with trees. It was a chair formed by a boulder framed by three slabs, and was reputed to have been blessed by St Patrick. The last inauguration it was used for was that of the great Hugh O'Neill, and in 1602 it was destroyed.

A stone in Ireland which still exists is St Columb's Stone, not far from Londonderry. This block $7\frac{1}{2}$ feet square has two depressions on it similar to footprints, and for his inauguration the chief of the O'Dohertys would stand upon the stone with bare feet and absorb the energies which pulsed forth.

Another famous stone has given its name to the town where it lies; this is the King's Stone at Kingston-upon-Thames which at one time was well beyond the boundaries of London but is now under threat of being engulfed by that monster metropolis. Here, from A.D. 900, seven Anglo-Saxon kings were crowned on the stone, which can be seen outside near the Guildhall.

In the City of London may be seen a similar stone, known as the London Stone, which was at one time set in a niche in the wall of St Swithin's church close to the Mansion House. This church was blitzed during the 1939–45 war, and when it was demolished in 1962 the stone and its iron grille were retained and placed in the wall on the edge of the pavement in Cannon Street on the same site. It may be seen dimly in its recess gracing the front of the Bank of China.

This is only a fragment of the original stone, which the sixteenth century antiquary John Stow described as being 'a great stone called London Stone, fixed in the ground very deep, fastened with bars of iron, and otherwise so stronglie set that if carts do runne against it through negligence the wheeles be broken, and the stone itself unshaken'. Although there is no tradition of it being used as a stone of initiation, the London Stone is of great antiquity and was held in veneration by the citizens who would make binding pacts across it and issue proclamations from it.

Colin Bord

London Stone   TQ 326809 (160)

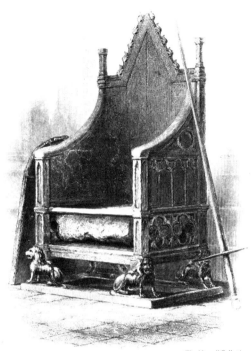

Coronation Stone, Westminster Abbey

On 16 February 1939, the psychometrist Olive Pixley, in the
presence of antiquarian researchers John Foster Forbes and
Major Tyler, and with the co-operation of the Abbey
authorities, recorded her impressions from the Coronation
Stone.

'*The stone is quite impersonal. I can get no history from it. It
has no power to absorb earth radiations, and is in a constant state of
transmission of cosmic energy. It is a meteorite. I get an instant
contact with a strong ray coming direct from the moon . . . pure
moon energy . . . The throne itself is vibrant with history – the
stone silent and remote.*'

Another holy stone, held in great veneration and also said
to be of meteoritic origin, is the black stone of the Kaaba, the
sacred shrine of the Mohammedans. It is placed in the
south-east wall of the great mosque of Mecca at such a height
that it may be kissed by devout pilgrims, and was said to
have been given to Abraham by Gabriel.

Janet Bord

The Nine Maidens, Boskednan, Cornwall
NG 434351 (189)

This small circle lies off the beaten track in an area of
lonely moorland untouched by civilization. The name
given to the circle is echoed elsewhere in the county, and
is explained by the legend that the nine maidens were
turned to stone for dancing on a Sunday (played to no
doubt by musicians such as the Blind Fiddler, illustrated
in this section, or the Pipers, who are now two standing
stones near Lamorna not far away).

Bowerman's Nose, near Manaton, Devon
SX 740805 (175)

This naturally weathered granite structure on the east of
Dartmoor looks for all the world like a huge figure
crouched up among the rocks, with only the stunted trees
for company.

There are more faces to be found in the photographs
in this section: look for the sharp-nosed laughing gnome
at Castlerigg, and the wise figure with eyes closed,
reclining in the avenue at Avebury . . . and maybe you
will find more. Who is to say that such faces are purely our
imagination, and that these stones were not at one time
endowed with lives of their own? Legends tell of men
transformed into standing stones, and think, too, of the
gigantic carved figures on Easter Island.

Kenneth Scowen

Ring of Brodgar, Stenness, Orkneys   HY 294133 (6)

This immense circle, with twenty-seven pillars still standing,
measures 340 feet across. There were originally around sixty
stones, and the tallest to be seen today is 15 feet high.

Lanyon Quoit, near Penzance, Cornwall   SW 430337 (189)

Lanyon Quoit is not now in its original form. It was
re-erected in 1815 or 1816 after falling during a storm. The
uprights may have been damaged, because originally it was
high enough for a man to pass underneath on horseback.
Traces of the earth mound which covered the stones can just
be seen close by.

35

the stone avenues of Carnac, France

At a time before history was written, the land of Britain did not end at Land's End, but continued westward and southward. The legends tell of a fair country of rolling green hills and clear waters where men lived at peace with the traditions of their fathers. This extensive land was Lyonesse, and stretched from Cornwall to include the Scilly Isles and southwards to Brittany, where on the south coast of the peninsula, overlooking the Bay of Biscay, was a great centre of subtle terrestrial energies. Here at Carnac the magicians of the ancient knowledge erected one of their most awe-inspiring temples.

The remnants of this magnificent structure can be seen scattered across the countryside, and today there are three separate groups of stones in the locality. The groups contain from ten to thirteen lines of stones, some over a mile long, the stones being placed at 15 foot intervals with 30 feet between the rows. Some of these huge unhewn rocks are 20 feet high and measure 20 or 30 feet round. It is thought that originally there were 1,000 rocks in each row, and that the three remaining groups were once part of a continuous structure, but many stones are now missing, having been broken up and used as building materials throughout the centuries.

When Lyonesse sank below the sea, this peninsula of land that now forms Brittany was left above water, as also were the Channel Islands and the Isles of Scilly. All these areas of land contain numerous relics of menhirs, dolmens and chambered tombs, erected several thousand years ago. Due to the remoteness of some of the islands, many of these have barely been recorded, and by no means thoroughly researched. On the Scilly Isles there are said to be three times as many megalithic structures as there are in the whole of Cornwall, which has a great abundance of them.

So great is the number of burial sites that it is probable that these islands were one of the groups used as 'The Isles of the Dead'. A similar group are the Flannan Isles which are off the west coast of Scotland, far beyond the Isle of Lewis, out in the storm-swept wastes of the Atlantic. These holy isles were the gateway to the next world to which the illustrious dead were ferried, and with solemn rites were buried amid the spirits of their forefathers.

That these have not always been islands is known by the remnants of civilization that have been seen awash at low tide, and the remains of buildings that can sometimes be seen through the clear water when the angle of the light is right. Off Brittany near Carnac is the island of Er-lanic, where there are the remnants of two stone circles on the shore which form a figure of eight stretching out to sea. The circle on the beach has 180 stones and can only be seen completely when the tide is out. One of its stones is 16 feet tall. The other circle is rarely uncovered by the waters. Legends tell of 140 churches that are lost beneath the waves. There is no doubt that the land has risen and fallen here in different ages; geologists have found beaches which were raised dozens of feet above high water mark, and some of these have later been returned to the sea level. There are also submerged forests to be found off the coast of Cornwall.

stones in Bradgate Park, near Loughborough, Leicestershire
SK 524116 (121)

Although there seems to be no archaeological record that these stones
represent an ancient sacred site, they look as though they were planted thus,
particularly the upright stone in the centre of the configuration. Charnwood
Forest, of which Bradgate Park is a part, is littered with rocks, but no stone
circles or standing stones have so far been identified there. In naturally rocky
areas, it is possible that some sacred sites would not be recognized as such
except by a sensitive.

one of the Devil's Arrows, near Boroughbridge, Yorkshire
SE 391666 (91)

Three stones called the Devil's Arrow form an alignment 570 feet long.
This photograph shows the most southerly, and tallest, arrow, $22\frac{1}{2}$ feet high.
The stones are of millstone grit quarried 6 miles away, and sixteenth century
records suggest that there were other stones here at that time. The
traditional explanation for the presence of these awe-inspiring monoliths
involves the Devil, who was angry with the people of the nearby town of
Aldborough. He went to the top of Howe Hill, and from there fired gigantic
arrows of stone, intending to demolish the town. As so often seemed to
happen, his ammunition missed its mark, and the Devil was thwarted again.

39

The Keswick Carles, Castlerigg, Cumberland
NY 292236 (82)

This circle of thirty-eight stones stands high up in the
mountains near Keswick, a most impressive spot in sunshine
or in mist. Iris Campbell's psychometric interpretation of
their purpose, made in 1944, is as follows:

*'These stones were part of a Memorial Assembly Place where
Kings came to mourn their Dead. A central Meeting Place where
Priests would come from surrounding Centres – but of a
funereal nature ; performing their funeral rites by weaving
different cosmic colours around the bier in order to speed the
departure of the passing Soul. It was only done for those of
higher grade of Priesthood so that they could be absolutely freed
for higher work elsewhere . . .'*

Rollright Stones, Oxfordshire   SP 296308 (145)

Although there are around seventy stones in the circle called the King's Men, it is said that they cannot be counted accurately. A few yards away stands a lone stone 8 feet high, called the King Stone, and a quarter of a mile away are the Whispering Knights, five stones possibly part of a burial chamber. A famous legend tells that all these stones were originally a king and his men (or in one version a general and his army) who were turned into stone by a witch (or a magician).

The capstone of the Whispering Knights was at one time dragged down the hill to be used as a bridge across a stream, but every night the stone moved, so it was dragged back up the hill again. More horses were needed to drag it down the hill than to drag it up! Yet another legend tells that the King Stone and the Whispering Knights go down the hill to drink from the stream at midnight.

The Whispering Knights, with the King's Men in the background

41

Giants' Graves, Whiting Bay, Isle of Arran   NS 043247 (66)

Beyond these stones, which are all that remain of an ancient
burial mound on one of Scotland's lonely and beautiful
islands, looms the dark hulk of Holy Isle.

Archaic Crosses and Carvings

Carvings on stones are the only 'written' records of prehistoric times, and their interpretation is by no means straightforward. The oldest carvings, such as those found in abundance at Newgrange (and also at other burial chambers, including Bryn-Celli-Ddu, Anglesey), show symbols rather than letters or words, and where symbols are concerned the interpretations can range from the idle doodling of workmen to theories involving mystical significance. Cup and ring markings evoke similarly wide-ranging theories, and what is proved by this is that we of the twentieth century find it very difficult to put ourselves in the place of those who executed such carvings, often very intricate and skilful, thousands of years ago. It is obvious that they were not made for fun – but why were they made? Pictish slabs or symbol stones are thought by some to have been tombstones, and if they were, these and the other early tombstones depicted in this section are far more beautiful and worthy of preservation than the stark and utilitarian erections we see today.

Strange carved figures, of uncertain date, are intriguing and could provide clues to the past. Some have withstood the weathering of centuries, so that the enigmatic faces can still be pondered over today; but who knows how many similar figures have not survived? Whatever field of prehistory concerns us, it is worth remembering that the relics to be seen today represent only a fraction of what must have originally existed. Many churches and other religious buildings bear strange carvings, on corbels, columns and doorways. Weird beasts and grimacing human faces peer down through the gloom which often hides them successfully unless the searcher knows where to look. The meaning behind these enigmatic figures can only be guessed at.

Sometimes identifiable writing has survived, such as the unusual Ogham alphabet; and, of more recent date, the inscriptions on early tombstones. However, there are many crosses which perhaps bear writings or messages which we have not yet recognized as such. An example is the typical interlaced Celtic design. It has been suggested that this may be a version of the twisting and knotting of cords used in various countries as a sacred 'language', and that what can be seen on Celtic crosses today is not merely intricate patterning. This theory could be extended, and it should be considered whether all pre-Christian stones bearing symbols and decorations may not in fact be covered in writing which holds some of the clues to take us a step further in our investigation into the nature of our ancestors.

More recent carvings, to be found in such places as on church walls and in caves, are not without interest, and may help to shed some light on the way the ordinary man was thinking (as opposed to the political or royal man's thoughts, of which 'history' is mainly composed). Sometimes these may show that pagan religious practices were not yet dead (as indeed they are not today, though they often go unrecognized – see 'The rites of spring and other pagan ceremonies'). Some examples of post-Roman carvings are as follows: the crude carvings possibly done in the thirteenth and fourteenth centuries in Royston Cave, Hertfordshire, showing religious figures such as the Crucifixion, St Christopher, St Catherine, etc.; the manticores (human-headed mythical animals) on church walls such as North Cerney church, Gloucestershire, and Old Byland church, Yorkshire; the carvings of various figures on Bidston Hill, Cheshire, depicted in this section.

The cross is an ancient symbol long pre-dating Christianity, and has appeared in many forms in different civilizations. (For an example, see Callanish in 'The standing stones and circles of prehistory'.) In Christianity, when it is associated, in the form of the crucifix, with the death of Christ, the cross is a symbol of misery and melancholy, but in earlier ages it symbolized the combining of God and Earth, and was a sign of harmony. The carved stone cross is still a living art form today, but those we see of the twentieth century are far removed from the first stone crosses, some of which are shown in this section. The most elaborate are certainly the Celtic crosses, particularly those found in Ireland; the most intriguing are probably the worn 'crosses' found everywhere in Cornwall, whose pattern and meaning may be pre-Christian.

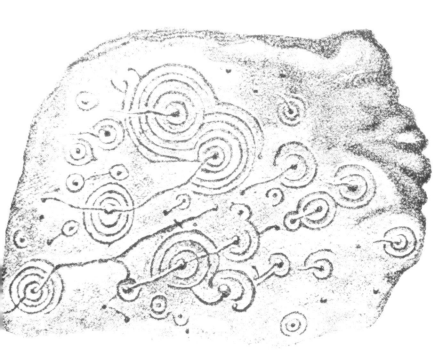

cup and ring marks at Old Bewick, Northumberland
NU 078216 (approx.) (71)

This engraving shows very clearly the carved cups and
concentric rings and channels which go by the name of 'cup
and ring marks'. They are found mainly on rocks in the north
of England, in Scotland and in Ireland, and their origin and
purpose remain obscure, although several theories have been
put forward to explain them.

One theory links them with mazes, which they resemble in
some ways (see 'The puzzle of the maze'); another suggests
that they were maps showing the locations of all the ancient
sites, earthworks, etc. in the area. Other interpretations
include: mortars for pounding roots, seeds, nuts or grain;
representations of the Sun, Moon and stars; dials for
marking time by the light of the Sun; part of a game which
was played; moulds for casting metal rings; indications of
sacrificial places; plans of burial mounds, the central hollow
being the actual burial place, the circles being standing
stones, ramparts, etc. surrounding the burial, and the
channel leading to the centre being the approach way,
entrance and tunnel into the mound.

cup and ring marks at Drumtroddan, near Port
William, Wigtownshire   NX 362444 (79)

John Foster Forbes believed that 'There is an affinity
between these cups and the nature of stars. A star is a
generator and transmitter of Cosmic Energy in spiral form.
These cups could be used as micro-cosmic examples of
spiral–staral energies.'

double-headed figure, Boa Island, Co. Fermanagh
H 085622 (N.I. 1″ map 4; Eire ½″ map 3)

This strange figure sits back-to-back with another. The
stone is 2½ feet high, and has a socket on top, and in this and
other respects has certain similarities to the figures found on
nearby White Island (illustrated elsewhere in this section).
This 'pagan Celtic god', as the figure has been described,
resides in the ancient graveyard of Caldragh on a small
island in Lower Lough Erne. Some Gaulish figures bear the
same sort of carving, and our mysterious 'god' is thought to
date from pre-Christian times.

Saxon crosses in the marketplace at Sandbach,
Cheshire   SJ 759608 (109)

Elaborately sculpted with Christian religious scenes,
animals, and scenes depicting the conversion to Christianity
in 653 A.D. of Peada of Mercia, these two old crosses have been
assigned dates between the seventh and ninth centuries.
The taller is nearly 17 feet high, the other 11 feet high, and
they did not originally stand together. They were smashed
by the Puritans in 1614, and the pieces were used for
various building purposes before they were finally collected
together again and re-erected in 1816.

48

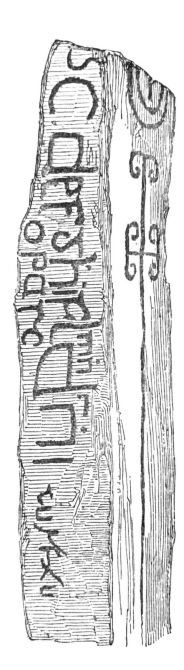

'alphabet stone', Kilmalkedar,
near Dingle, Co. Kerry
Q 403062 (Eire ½″ map 20)

Now standing in the churchyard
and in use as a gravestone, this
ancient stone has an alphabet carved
on it. This may have been done for
teaching purposes in early Christian
times.

49

Bidston Hill, Cheshire   SJ 286897 (100)

Near Birkenhead, on a flat sandstone outcrop by the
Observatory, are several carvings of figures. This photograph
shows part of the body of a supposed Sun goddess (note the
Sun symbol at her feet). In her right hand she holds
something which may be a large key or a cloak, but this is
not shown in the photograph. The figure is about 4½ feet
long, and faces north of east. There is also a carving of a
cat-headed Moon goddess, with a Moon symbol at her feet.
Although these carvings must have been renewed over the
years, they are thought to have originated with the Norse-
Irish, who settled here around A.D. 1000.

50

Bidston Hill, Cheshire

This horse is around 12 feet long, and faces exactly towards
the Midsummer sunrise. On his neck is what may be a Sun
symbol; the outlines have been chalked in so that they can be
more clearly seen. (See 'Hill figures – signals to the gods?',
and note the similarities between such carvings as this and
the larger white horses cut in the chalk.) Although the
present figure only dates back to the eighteenth century,
there are signs that an earlier carving was renewed.

Also on the rock at Bidston Hill are depicted human
figures which possibly represent the Mummers' Play
performed near here until quite recently. These carvings are
also eighteenth century.

51

St Patrick's cross, Cashel, Co. Tipperary   S 073407
(Eire $\frac{1}{2}''$ map 18)

This mid-twelfth century cross stands on the Rock of
Cashel, in the cemetery adjacent to Cormac's Chapel. (For
more details of the buildings on this site, see 'The sanctity of
ancient sites'.) It has the crucifixion on one side and S^t
Patrick on the other, with geometrical designs on the base.
These designs could have more than merely decorative
significance.

St Piran's cross, Penhale Sands, Perranzabuloe,
Cornwall   SW 772564 (185)

One of many shaped standing stones, called 'crosses',
in the county, this one stands on a long stretch of
sandhills, under which is said to be buried the large
city of Langarrow. Over 1,000 years ago, because of
the wickedness of the inhabitants, a violent storm
arose which lasted for three days and nights, causing
the entire city and its people to be buried beneath the
sand. This may be a legend, but in 1835 the shifting
sands revealed a buried church.

   The age of the Cornish crosses is uncertain, but
some are thought to be pre-Christian, and to show
Egyptian influence. The shape, with a round head, and
two side projections above a tapering base, echoes the
shape of the Egyptian ankh, symbol of life.

Egyptian ankh

53

doorway, St Kevin's church, Glendalough, Co.
Wicklow   T 126968 (approx.) (Eire ½″ map 16)

This blocked-up doorway also echoes the ankh shape,
and has been included here for comparison. The church
is ninth century or even older, and stands on an ancient
and important monastic site. (For more information on
Glendalough, see 'The sanctity of ancient sites'.)

cross at St Buryan, near Penzance, Cornwall
SW 409256 (approx.) (189)

This Cornish cross dates from the fifth or sixth century.
Many such crosses are really ancient sacred stones which
have been Christianized by the addition of a cross in
later ages.

Treslea Down cross, Cardinham, Cornwall   SX 130688
(approx.) (186)

Most of the Cornish crosses are to be found by the roadside,
such as this small example which is only 2 feet high.

Janet Bord

cross outside the church of St Michael and all Angels, Bosherston, Pembrokeshire   SR 966948 (138/151)

A face is carved on the head of this cross, which was found by the villagers after the Dissolution of the Monasteries in the sixteenth century. They could not find the stem, so they placed the head on a locally-hewn upright (a sacred standing stone?) and erected the cross on two tiers of steps to serve as a preaching cross.

Newgrange, Co. Meath,   O 007727 (Eire ½″ map 13)

Newgrange is one of the finest examples of a passage grave in Western Europe, and was probably erected around 2500 B.C. It is famous for its many decorated stones, some of which are shown here. Spirals, lozenges, cup and ring marks, and other geometrical designs can be seen on the large stones round the base of the mound, as well as on the stones inside the chambers. The mound consisted of a cairn of pebbles, with white quartz stones on the outer surface.

The designs on the stones are probably symbolic, not just decorative, and the spirals may represent the maze of life (see also 'The puzzle of the maze'). Also, compare these designs with those carved on the pillars inside Durham Cathedral, illustrated in 'The sanctity of ancient sites'.

The kings of Tara were buried here, according to legend. Newgrange, which is one of many burial mounds in the pagan cemetery of Brug-Na-Boinne, also has associations with the Tuatha de Danann, ancient rulers of Ireland, of whom Dagda, Lug the Irish Sun-god, and others were buried in this important and remarkable area.

a stone fom the outer kerb

Newgrange, Co. Meath   O 007727 (Eire ½″ map 13)

This highly worked entrance slab is 10½ feet long and 4½ feet
high. Shown here half buried in the ground, as it was before
the recent excavations, only four of the five complete spirals
can be seen. The incomplete spirals are not the result of
damage, but were originally executed as they are seen here,
to cover the entire surface of the unhewn stone.

Celtic carved cross, Carew, Pembrokeshire
SN 047037 (138/151)

This well-preserved cross shows a variety of designs. On the
top panel is the swastika, a Sanskrit word which means
well-being. The swastika has always been known as a
symbol of good luck. It is also a Sun symbol, and has been
found in Hindu carvings, in South American rock carvings,
and on Central American mound builders' pottery. The
bottom panel shows an interlaced strap design of great
ingenuity. It is a continuous ribbon without any ends, and if
traced round will return the explorer to his starting point.
Was this more than just an intricate piece of design? Did it
convey a message to the initiated when it was originally
carved?

Bennett's cross, near Postbridge, Devon
SX 653793 (approx.) (188)

Cormac's Chapel, Rock of Cashel,
Co. Tipperary
S 073407 (Eire ½″ map 18)

This chapel is rich in strange carvings –
beasts and monsters, human heads,
shapes and patterns. Here a centaur is
shooting an arrow at a lion, which is
itself clawing at some small creature.
This carving is on the lintel of the richly
ornamented north doorway. Does the
figure described as a centaur have any
connection with the Sagittarius figure?

Ogham stone, Teampull Geal, Ballymorereagh, Co. Kerry

Ogham stones are found mainly in southern Ireland, Scotland, and south Wales, with a few examples in south-west England. Ogham is a script in which the letters of the Roman alphabet are represented by short strokes, the number of strokes in a group and their position on one side of or across a central line, usually the edge of a standing stone, representing a certain letter. It is thought to have developed in early Christian times, and although it is not really clear why it was developed, it was later used for writing epitaphs. In some circles, the origin of the Ogham characters has been attributed to the Druids. Its use declined in the seventh century A.D.

This example, to be found on the Dingle Peninsula of south-west Ireland, stands near St Monachan's oratory, and is said to mark his grave. The Ogham inscription reads QENILOCI MAQ I MAQ I AINIA MUC; there is a simple cross on each side and a Latin inscription reads FECT QUENILOC (made by Qeniloc).

Colin Bord

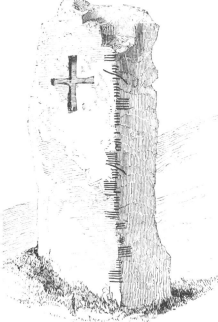

Ogham stone, Caldey Island, Pembrokeshire   SS 141962 (152)

The church of St Illtud on the small, monastic island of Caldey, houses this stone. It is thought to date from the sixth century A.D., and a fragmentary inscription in Ogham can be seen round the top. There is also a Latin inscription, possibly contemporary with the Ogham inscription or possibly added later. Many Ogham stones were later 'Christianized' by the addition of a cross and a Latin inscription.

61

'weeping cross', Ampney Crucis, near Cirencester,
Gloucestershire   SP 065019 (157)

This strange stone erection was probably a 'weeping cross',
the 'place to which penitents resorted to bemoan over their
shortcomings'. It stands in the village churchyard; the head
was replaced in 1860 after being found in some rubble in the
rood loft of the church, where it was probably hidden to
avoid destruction by the Puritans. It is interesting to
compare this cross-head with that of the Monasterboice
cross depicted elsewhere in this section.

Edna Knowles

gravestone at Penmachno, Caernarvonshire
SH 790506 (107)

This fifth century gravestone bears a chi-rho monogram (the first letters of the Greek *Christos*, or Christ), one of very few examples in Britain. The inscription reads CARAUSIUS/ HIC IACIT/IN HOC CON/ GERIES LA/PIDUM (Here lies Carausius in this heap of stones). The stone was found in a field near Penmachno, but is now in the parish church.

Clonmacnoise, near Athlone, Co. Offaly
N 010306 (Eire ½″ map 15)

At this important monastic site are a large number of artistic grave-slabs, dating from the eighth to twelfth centuries. The one illustrated shows an elaborate cross with an inscription reading A PRAYER FOR MAELFINNIA. Maelfinnia was probably the abbot of that name who died in 991 or 992.

Clonmacnoise, near Athlone,
Co. Offaly
N 010306 (Eire ½″ map 15)

This tombstone was originally a quern
or hand millstone. It is ornamented,
and bears the single name
SECHNASACH, who may have been a
priest who died around 928 A.D.

Runic characters spell out the word
JISLHEaRD on this early (ninth or
tenth century) coffin-stone which was
found in the marketplace in Dover,
Kent. The first character is not a rune
but the Christian cross, and may
indicate the Christian burial of a Viking
warrior. Runes were a script used by the
Norsemen and considered to have
magical properties. Runic characters
could be used for divination by the
initiated, to help or harm others, obtain
victory and cure disease.

cross in Sancreed churchyard, Cornwall
SW 420294 (189)

This 9 feet high cross shows a fleur-de-lis (or a spearhead –
opinions differ) rising from a chalice, and has a sixth century
inscription.

Pictish symbol stone at Glamis Manse, near Forfar,
Angus NO 385466 (50)

These carved stones are found only in north and east
Scotland. The earliest ones are thought to pre-date
Christian influence, but the actual dating varies according to
the authority consulted, from the fifth century to the ninth
century A.D. The later slabs depict Christian symbols, and
by the end of the tenth century the older symbols had died
out. The designs most frequently seen include living
creatures (animals, birds, snakes, fishes); objects such as
mirrors, combs and swords; and geometrical shapes. Some
of the designs are thought to have been influenced by early
Christian manuscript and decorative work. It has been
suggested that the stones were intended as tombstones.
   This photograph shows the back of an elaborately
decorated stone – on the front is an intricate cross,
surrounded by the figures of men and animals, and symbols.
This stone stands nearly 9 feet high.

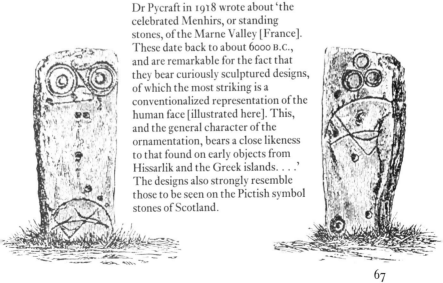

Dr Pycraft in 1918 wrote about 'the
celebrated Menhirs, or standing
stones, of the Marne Valley [France].
These date back to about 6000 B.C.,
and are remarkable for the fact that
they bear curiously sculptured designs,
of which the most striking is a
conventionalized representation of the
human face [illustrated here]. This,
and the general character of the
ornamentation, bears a close likeness
to that found on early objects from
Hissarlik and the Greek islands. . . .'
The designs also strongly resemble
those to be seen on the Pictish symbol
stones of Scotland.

67

Muiredach's cross, Monasterboice, Co. Louth
O 043821 (Eire ½″ map 13)

Muiredach was abbot of Monasterboice monastery from
890–923, and this elaborately carved cross dates from the
tenth century. It shows scriptural and other scenes, which
would originally have been coloured. The summit is shaped
as a shingle-roofed church, and the whole cross stands 17
feet 8 inches tall. On the left is a ruined round tower. (For
more information on round towers, see 'Ancient buildings
and other stone structures'.)

carved figures on White Island, Co. Fermanagh
H 173600 (N.I. 1″ map 4; Eire ½″ map 3)

The date of these figures is doubtful, but dates ranging from the eighth to the twelfth centuries have been put forward. Their significance is also uncertain, but two are thought to represent bishops with croziers; a warrior and a sheila-na-gig (an erotic female figure) have also been identified. The carving of the eight figures, which are 2 to 4½ feet in height, has affinities to Gaulish work, and the full-length figures have sockets in the tops of their heads, as if they were intended to carry some kind of superstructure.

The carvings were originally in an earlier monastic building on the island (which is in Castle Archdale Bay, in Lower Lough Erne), but in the twelfth century were hidden in the church where they now stand, because they were felt to have pagan affinities which were embarrassing to the Christians. The church is now a roofless single cell.

cross at Aycliffe, Durham   NZ 285225 (approx.) (85)

Of uncertain date, but thought to be between the eighth and eleventh centuries, this cross displays ornamentation which shows an Irish influence in the familiar twisting and knotting. The creature at the bottom of the design is called an Agnus Dei, or Lamb of God, but compare him with the carving of a centaur in Cormac's Chapel, Rock of Cashel, illustrated elsewhere in this section.

Earthworks
on the Hilltops

'*Of all the many thousands of earth-works of various
kinds to be found in England, those about which
anything is known are very few, those of which there
remains nothing more to be known scarcely exist . . .
Within them lie hidden all the secrets of time before
history begins, and by their means only can that history be
put into writing : they are the back numbers of the
island's story, as yet unread, much less indexed.*'

A. Hadrian Allcroft in *Earthwork of England*

Across the face of Britain there are some 40,000 mounds of earth, a
mysterious legacy left to us by our early forebears, and there may be
thousands more that are unrecorded or now obliterated by time and
man. Many of these mounds contain burials, and range in size from the
largest such as Newgrange, a mound 45 feet high containing a chamber
20 feet high (see 'Archaic crosses and carvings'), down to round barrows that are barely noticeable from ground level, only 15 feet across
and 2 or 3 feet high, though they do show up in aerial photographs.
Others were never used for burials, but were the sacred meeting places
or moot or toot mounds for a locality. Perhaps the supreme example of
this is Silbury Hill, although it is not certain yet what its original purpose was. But there are many smaller examples of these to be found
throughout the land, Merlin's Mount and Tynwald Hill being two that
are illustrated here.

Both burial mounds and moot mounds frequently have stories and
legends attached to them which indicate the awe and respect in which
they have been held by men through the ages. Many of these legends
feature giants or fairies, and had we the time to delve deep enough, they
might provide us with clues for the reasons behind the construction of
some of the more enigmatic mounds.

One such story concerns a hill called The Wrekin, near Shrewsbury,
Shropshire, which has on its prominent summit an ancient enclosure
or hillfort. A Welsh giant had quarrelled with the mayor of Shrewsbury
and was carrying a spade of earth with which to dam the river Severn

and thereby flood the town. But he lost his way, and asked a passing cobbler, who immediately realized that the giant was up to no good. He showed him the bag of old shoes which he had to mend, and said he had worn them all out since he left Shrewsbury, it was so far away. The giant, who was feeling tired, immediately threw down the soil he was carrying, and it became the Wrekin. Nearby Wenlock Edge was formed where the giant wiped his boots. Similar stories are told of Maes Knoll, an earthwork in Somerset, of Silbury Hill, and other hills and mounds.

Many long barrows are reputed to have giants buried in them, and the name 'giant' is often used, as in Giant's Grave near Milton Lilbourne, Wiltshire; Giant's Grave at Holcombe, Somerset; and the Giant's Hills near Skendleby, Lincolnshire. There are also traditions that when opened some of these long barrows have disclosed the skeletons of giant men 8 feet tall or more. Was there really a race of giants in this land at one time? Or could there have been a race of people with gigantic mental abilities who perhaps possessed as a matter of course the faculties that we term ESP, together with the ability to levitate large masses of matter and control the currents of wind and weather?

In many parts of Britain the round barrows were the traditional home of the fairy folk, and were therefore avoided by the country people. Such places as Fairy Toot in Somerset, the barrow called Elf Howe near Folkton, Yorkshire, and a round barrow at Beedon in Berkshire, were said to be inhabited by fairies. Cornwall has always been a stronghold of fairy lore, and on a fine night it is said that they can be seen dancing on top of the chambered round barrow of Carn Gluze, near St Just.

The long barrows have always been a source of puzzlement to students of archaeology. These great mounds of earth, some over 300 feet long, often set on prominent hilltops, have been found to contain burials, usually within a stone chamber at one end, the rest of the mound being apparently nothing but earth. Some mounds were reopened at a later date and more interments placed within, or in some cases these later burials were placed in the sides of the sacred mounds. Just as our great abbeys and cathedrals contain many monuments and burials of great men but were not built primarily for this purpose, so perhaps the long barrows were caused to be built for reasons other than those of interment of the dead. Were they perhaps part of a worldwide system of planetary engineering which modified and directed some subtle form of beneficial energy which was thought to flow through the land?

Other investigators have noted the similarity between the great length of the barrows with the small human figure at one end, and the vast length of a twentieth century space rocket with its comparatively tiny human figures in the nose section. Could these long barrows be a form of imitative magic directed to the sky gods? Were there beings who had contacted earthmen in past ages and whose superior intellect and technology caused their memory to be venerated by the peoples of the Neolithic Age? And was an attempt to regain the lost knowledge and assistance that these beings from the stars had been able to bestow the cause of the enigmatic shape of the long barrows? These are not the wild speculations of immature minds, but have been proposed by sane and serious people in recent years.

There has also been noted a similarity between the shapes of earthworks and the commonly reported shapes of UFOs (unidentified flying objects), which were first popularly called flying saucers. Some round barrows are termed 'saucer' because of their prevalent shape, others are known as 'disc' and 'bell' barrows. These three terms have all been applied to UFOs when sightings have been reported by people who probably had no knowledge of the terms used by archaeologists and were certainly not trying to make any such comparisons. Other UFOs have been reported of a huge size and tubular shape. These are thought by some to be 'mother ships', used by the smaller saucers as a mobile base, and they have been compared by some with long barrows.

Perhaps the 'cargo cults' of the islands of Melanesia in the Pacific can give a present-day parallel to the thinking behind the building of the barrows and other mounds. Here the islanders clear landing strips, make large wooden models of aircraft and erect red crosses, all in an attempt to persuade the same aircraft to land which they have seen provide the white man with abundant goods for his material wellbeing. Is it possible that craft from civilizations beyond the confines of our planet have paid us visits in distant ages, and that the barrow builders were trying to bring the sky gods back to earth again?

Many of these ancient sites have been considered sacred throughout the ages, and have been used in succeeding ages for burials and religious practices. On Jersey, in the Channel Islands, is a 40 feet high man-made mound named La Hougue Bie. On its summit are two tiny chapels of early date. In 1924 excavations were made into the side of the mound and a great Neolithic tomb was uncovered. Seventy huge stones were used in its construction, some weighing 30 tons, and forming a passage with four chambers at the end. This was one of the most impressive discoveries of its kind, but the wealth of archaeological finds that was hoped for was absent. Only the scattered bones of eight people and a few beads were found: the Vikings, who frequently raided the islands and were noted for their grave-robbing activities, had been there first.

Unique in Britain is the Meayll Circle, which stands just below the summit of Mull Hill, Cregneish, on the Isle of Man. This consists of six chambers set round the circumference of a circle in two groups of three. The chambers are made from large slabs of local slate 8 feet by 3 feet and 6 inches thick. Although there is no roof on the structure now, it is probable that there was originally. In 1897 when it was first excavated, twenty-six burial urns were found, but these are not necessarily of the same date. One curious feature was the large number of white quartz pebbles that were found on the floors. Within the stone chambers of some of the mounds opened, the remains of bodies have been found sitting propped against the interior walls, suggesting that this position had been consciously adopted and was not a burial. Perhaps those whose hour had come would enter the tumulus through the low entrance passage, there to await their transition to the realms of the next life.

Many different names are used for these earthworks, depending on which part of the country they are found in. Examples are tumulus, how, low, tump, butt, toot, tot, cop, mount, hill, knoll. Sometimes one of these words forms part of a name, and place names often hold clues to the area's history, e.g. Drakelow (Derbyshire) means 'dragon's mound'. Earthworks and mounds are also frequently indicated by the name endings 'bury' from the Old English 'burh', or 'borough' from the Old English 'beorg', e.g. Modbury, Dorset ('mod' was probably 'mot' or 'moot', i.e. a moot-mound or meeting place) and Hillborough, Kent ('hill', in this instance, was originally 'halig' meaning 'holy'). Around one quarter of the 40,000 barrows in England are on the Yorkshire Moors. Thousands more have disappeared under the plough throughout Britain, but even these can sometimes be seen from the air. Slight elevations in the ground show up in slanting sunlight, or the texture of the soil affects the moisture content and causes differences in plant growth, the resulting patterns being distinguishable from above.

Another mystery bequeathed to us, even more impressive than the mounds, is the meaning of the great enclosures on the hilltops encircled by one or more earthen banks and ditches. There are about 1,500 of these in England, and although they are often conventionally termed

74

Iron Age hillforts, there are many today who doubt that this was their original date or use. It is also suspected that the people of the Iron Age may simply have made modifications to the earthworks, in an attempt to turn them into defensive structures. What, then, could have been their initial purpose? Why did the men of prehistory expend such huge amounts of time and energy in moving vast quantities of earth to re-shape the hilltops? Why did they build miles of sinuous dykes across country? And what was the purpose of those curious constructions known as cursús? There is a cursús just north of Stonehenge which is formed by two parallel banks of earth 100 yards apart running for $1\frac{3}{4}$ miles across country. The banks are curved round to meet and close up at each end. In Dorset there is a similar construction, but this is even larger, the banks being 270 feet apart and 6 miles in length.

Very little evidence has been found to show that the interiors of the hillforts were occupied to any great extent, and such as there is points to a time considerably later than that of the original construction, so the theory that they were the defensive dwelling places of tribal groups is an unlikely one. As defensive positions they were often of an impracticable design. Uffington Castle, which is on the hilltop above the white horse, has ditches and banks of such slight contour that it is hard to believe that they were dug to be defensive positions, even allowing for the erosion and sedimentation of centuries. At the other extreme there is Maiden Castle in Dorset. This great work of prehistoric engineering covers an area of 120 acres, and it has been estimated that it would require a quarter of a million men to defend it effectively!

Why, then, were these constructions made? By looking at the names, legends, and traditions attached to these sites we may find some answers. The name 'Maiden' is frequently connected with ancient stones, as in the 'Nine Maidens' (see 'The standing stones and circles of pre-history'), and Maiden Ways or Lanes are found leading to the places where the rites to the mother goddess figure were enacted. In Uffington Castle there is a traditional celebration or 'pastime' connected with the seven-yearly scouring of the white horse (see 'Hill figures – signals to the gods?'). It is very possible that this dates back to prehistoric times when it was not only a jollification but also a solemn rite (see 'The rites of spring and other pagan ceremonies'). Other earthworks are associated with ball games on Palm Sunday (Cley Hill, Wiltshire, and Martinsell Hill, Wiltshire), there was horse racing at Lambert's Castle in Dorset, and sheep fairs at Yarnbury and Woodbury Camps (see information on fairs in 'The rites of spring and other pagan ceremonies').

These are some of the many clues that suggest to us that the ancient men built upon the hills not for reasons of war but because the re-moulding of the countryside was an integral part of their way of life; that by sculpturing the forms of the hills and downs they could enhance and magnify those currents of natural energies that flowed, and still do flow, through the body of the earth, and by the use of sound, movement, and above all thought, in the form of solemn and joyful ceremonies they could manipulate the vibrations in order to bring the bountiful and vital life force flowing through the land and the people.

The slope of Silbury Hill, showing a notch near the top, just below the summit.

Colin Bord

Silbury Hill, near Marlborough, Wiltshire   SU 100685 (157)

130 feet high, covering an area of $5\frac{1}{4}$ acres, and with a diameter of just over 100 feet across its flat top, Silbury Hill is the largest prehistoric man-made mound in Europe. The reason for its construction is still unknown, despite several official excavations, though the most popular archaeological theory is that it was a gigantic burial mound, possibly for an important personage. Legend tells how King Sil was buried there on horseback (other versions tell of a lifesize figure of solid gold, or a man in golden armour on horseback, or a king buried in a golden coffin), but so far no trace of any burial has been found inside the mound, except for a comparatively recent one on the top.

Andrew Davidson, in an article in *Britain : A Study in Patterns*, tells of the theory of a researcher at the turn of the century, Moses B. Cotsworth, who believed that Silbury was 'a gigantic sun-dial to determine the seasons and the true length of the year', and that the legend of King Sil (i.e., the Sun), the old zodiac of ten signs, and the Glastonbury zodiac (see 'Glastonbury's Temple of the Stars and other zodiacs') all tie in with his theory.

The impression of psychometrist Olive Pixley, when she visited the hill with John Foster Forbes, was that the mound was erected in order to cover a stone circle. Black magic had been practised there, with the result that the place had so evil an atmosphere and effect that the only way to counteract this was to destroy the circle and bury the stones. During an excavation in 1849, stones were reported to have been found, and the most recent investigation (in 1968–9 organized by BBC-2 under the direction of Professor Richard Atkinson) resulted in the discovery of a random distribution of isolated boulders and small groups of up to four stones, though all were relatively small. New radio-carbon dating during this investigation resulted in the construction of Silbury Hill being dated to around 2750 B.C., which is earlier than was previously thought. No further evidence was discovered concerning the purpose of the mound, and Silbury remains a mystery still.

Silbury on a cold, wintry day, seen from halfway up the hill on the top of which stands West Kennet long barrow (illustrated elsewhere in this section).

Colin Bord

Northern Ireland Tourist Board

Ballymacdermot single-court grave, near Newry,
Co. Armagh   J 063238

Standing 600 feet up in the hills, this burial site affords a fine
view across the surrounding countryside. Many other burial
mounds are found in similar locations.

Badbury Rings, near Wimborne Minster, Dorset
ST 964030 (179)

Three outer banks wind round this pine-topped hill, like a
coiled serpent, and when seen from the air they are very
reminiscent of the ritual mazes that are thought to have been
part of the pre-Christian rites. Badbury Rings is one of the
most spectacular earthworks in the county of Dorset, and the
two entrances face east and west as in so many of these sites,
more suggestive of ceremonial than defensive purposes.

Attributed to the Iron Age, the site has never been
excavated, and it is most likely to be very much older.
Roman roads meet here, and this earthwork was once the
seat of an ancient moot, where the chieftains of the locality
would meet to legislate.

Devil's Dyke, Wheathampstead, Hertfordshire
TL 184135 (147)

This dyke and another called the Slad, a little to the east, are
thought to have formed one earthwork covering some 100
acres. Devil's Dyke is about 40 feet deep and 90 feet wide,
with a 9 foot bank on one side and a 6 foot bank on the other.
 The earthwork is thought to be the site of Julius Caesar's
attack in 54 B.C. on the tribal headquarters of Cassivellaunus.
It is hard to believe that this place might once have been the
scene of violence and bloodshed, for all is now peaceful under
an arch of noble trees.

West Kennet long barrow, Wiltshire   SU 104677 (157)

This impressive burial mound stands within the complex of
ancient structures around Avebury, from which site it is 1½
miles distant. The mound itself, of chalk, is 330 feet long and
8 to 10 feet high, and at the eastern end covers a 40 foot long
burial chamber built of sarsen boulders. According to radio-
carbon dating, the barrow was built around 2500 B.C., and it
is thought to have been still used for burial purposes for the
next 1,000 years or so. Around 1600 B.C., the entrance was
finally blocked by a huge stone 12 feet high.

These huge stones were used to block the entrance to the tomb when it was finally sealed. Before 1956 they were leaning out of position or fallen, and in that year were re-erected in their original socket holes. To the left, the beginning of the mound, which stretches back 330 feet, can be seen.

Some of the stones inside the burial chamber, seen from inside the furthest of the five chambers which lead off from the central passage, looking along the passage towards the entrance stone.

Colin Bord

Geoffrey N. Wright

84

The Tor, Glastonbury, Somerset   ST 513386 (165)

'The Tor is a strange hill, and it is hard to believe that its form is wholly the work of Nature. Round it winds a spiral way in three great coils, which was beyond all question a processional way. When did the Christians worship upon high places? Never. But such mounts as this were always sacred to the sun.'

Dion Fortune in *Avalon of the Heart*

The old gods have never relinquished their hold upon the Tor. Although the great stones of the Sun circle, that legend says stood upon its summit, were cast down and used in the foundations of Glastonbury Abbey, and upon its summit a church dedicated to the serpent-slaying St Michael was erected, they waited for their time to come. In A.D. 1000 there was an earthquake which reduced the Christian cruciform church to a pile of rubble and left standing only the tower, a pagan monolith. Excavations were carried out on the Tor in 1967, and the foundations of a church were found, together with cells and what may have been a chieftain's residence.

At the base of the Tor a number of saints had their hermitages by the holy well. One of these was St Collen. He overheard two men speaking of the fairies who lived on the Tor, and forbade them to speak of these beings, who he said were devils. The men warned him that the King of the Fairies would not overlook such an insult. Later the saint was invited to visit the King on the Tor. He went, and as a precaution carried a flask of holy water beneath his cloak. At the top of the Tor was the palace, glittering with lights and thronged with richly dressed people moving about to the sound of sweet melodies. The King invited St Collen to join him at his banquet. 'I do not eat the leaves of a tree,' replied the saint, and threw the holy water over the heads of the company. Of an instant the music and the lights faded, the company shimmered like a haze and faded into the mists of the night, and the saint was alone on the windy hilltop.

In 1945 John Foster Forbes, antiquarian, and Iris Campbell, psychometrist, visited the Tor to record the impressions that Miss Campbell could receive, in order to throw more light on its early history. They found that the rites being practised there were designed to restore bird and flower life forms to a more complete condition. They had become greatly impaired due to the succession of natural calamities that had befallen the earth. The ritual involved a dance of circular motion, moving sunwise and upwards round the spiral path. A tremendous vortex of power was produced which, on an etheric level, created a canopy of a 'glazed substance'. This could act as a receiving centre for the absorption and refraction of regenerative forces to which the bird and flower life could respond. (The Tor is described further in 'Glastonbury's Temple of the Stars and other zodiacs'.)

Tynwald Hill, St John's, Isle of Man   SC 278819 (87)

A present-day ceremony with its roots in pagan times can be
witnessed every 5 July (old Midsummer Day) on the Isle of
Man. The site is a four-tiered conical mound of earth, and
during the Tynwald ceremony the laws passed during the
previous year are read out to the assembled populace in
English and the island's own ancient language of Manx.
Before this, however, there is a service in the nearby St
John's church, and as the day is a national holiday, a fair is
held on the green. Churches dedicated to St John the
Baptist, whose feast day was celebrated on Midsummer Day,
generally indicate that pagan Midsummer fire festivals were
long ago practised there. (See 'The rites of spring and other
pagan ceremonies'.)

Trencrom Hill, near Lelant, Cornwall   SW 518362 (189)

The summit of this rocky hill is known to have been occupied because traces of hut-circles have been found, and a massive rampart using the natural rock formations. But who lived there? According to the legends they were ill-tempered giants who hid their treasure in the hill, where it is now guarded by spriggans (the ghosts of giants, found only among the ancient stones up on the moorlands). Two hundred years ago, a tin miner, greedy for gold, crept up the hill one night when he saw lights among the rocks. He found the entrance to a long passage, down which he could see spirits dancing, the giants' treasure unguarded. He managed to grab a little of the gold and escape with it, a feat very rarely rivalled for the spriggans were not easily tricked.

87

Janet Bord

Beacon Hill, near Woodhouse Eaves, Leicestershire   SK 509148 (121)

818 feet high, the top of this hill, which is the second highest in the county, can be seen on the left of the picture. Evidence of the prehistoric occupation of this excellent vantage point can be found in the remains of an Iron Age hillfort, and the name of the hill suggests that it was once also used as a beacon site. It is said to be haunted by the ghost of a monk with a skeletal face, accompanied by a dog, a ghost story which sounds like a legend from the past, pointing to earlier activities on the hill.

Wansdyke, near Marlborough, Wiltshire   SU 127652 (157)

Thought to have been built during the sixth century A.D. as a defensive frontier, the ramparts of this great dyke stretch across Somerset and Wiltshire, although it is not continuous. The name Wansdyke derives from that of the Anglo-Saxon god Woden (*Wodens dic*), who was an important deity to the early English. Many earthworks elsewhere in the country are called Grimsdyke; Grim the 'masked one' was another form of Woden.

   Although given a sixth century date, could this earthwork be of pre-Christian date? Stretching as it does across the southern edge of the Avebury/Silbury complex, it could possibly have some connection with that important site.

88

Edna Knowles

Capel Garmon burial chamber,
Denbighshire   SH 818543 (107)

This burial chamber has lost part of its
covering mound of earth or stones, with
the result that the details of its
construction can be more easily seen.
The site is fairly high up, with a clear
view of the surrounding countryside,
as is so often the case.

Merlin's Mount, Marlborough, Wiltshire   SU 183686 (157)

Five miles east of Avebury is this terraced moot mound, known locally as
Merlin's Mount. The rural setting has now been replaced by the buildings
of Marlborough College, within the grounds of which it stands. The distinct
terraces are reminiscent of Tynwald Hill on the Isle of Man (illustrated
elsewhere in this section), which is still in use.

On the hillside above is cut a white horse of crude outline. This is of no
very great age; it is generally agreed that it was cut in 1804 by the scholars of
Mr Greasley's Academy, a local educational establishment.

Maes Howe chambered tomb, near Stromness, Orkney   HY 317127 (6)

Beneath a 24 foot high mound of clay and stones is a stone chamber 15 feet
square. The entrance is through a 36 foot long passage lined with slabs of
stone averaging 18½ feet in length. In this photograph we see one corner
of the chamber which clearly shows the elegant use of natural undressed
stone on the corbelled roof. Each corner has a supporting pillar. The wall
opposite the entrance and the two side walls each have a recess leading into
the body of the earthen mound. Burials may have been placed within these
recesses. On the floor in front of each opening there is a massive wedge of
stone which was originally used for blocking the entrance to each recess.

From the time it was finally sealed, about 1500 B.C., this tomb, if that is
what it was, remained undisturbed until A.D. 1150 when some Norse pirates
who were spending the winter on the island broke into the tomb. They left
nothing but some runic inscriptions testifying to their presence. (For more
information on runes, see 'Archaic crosses and carvings'.)

British Crown Copyright: reproduced by permission of the Department of the Environ

Five Knolls, Dunstable, Bedfordshire   TL 007210 (147)

The Dunstable Downs seem to reach up to the sky, and
these tumuli are perched right on the top. Our ancestors
loved the high places of the earth both in life and for their
final resting places. Burials have been found in those
barrows which have been excavated here, and these mounds
may date from around 1500 B.C.

Carn Brea, near Redruth, Cornwall   SW 685407 (189)

Hut sites have been identified on this 36-acre hillfort and
dated to the Iron Age, though Neolithic pottery and
flintwork also discovered suggest that the site was occupied
even earlier. Within the walls of the hillfort are the ruins of
a castle of the twelfth to eighteenth centuries.

94

Burrough Hill, near Melton Mowbray, Leicestershire
SK 761119 (122)

The ramparts on the skyline enclose a roughly rectangular
area of around 12 acres. The site is called a hillfort and is
thought to have been constructed in the first century B.C.
Pottery and bones found inside the camp indicate that the
site was occupied for several hundred years, and it may have
been the tribal capital of the Coritani, although no traces of
huts or other buildings have been found.

Camster cairn, near Watten, Caithness
ND 260440 (16)

This cairn, which with its neighbour forms the Grey Cairns
of Camster, has a bleak and lonely outlook high above the
surrounding plains. Below the loose stones is a burial
chamber where the remains of cremations have been found.

95

Maiden Castle, near Dorchester, Dorset   SY 669884 (178)

This aerial view of Maiden Castle gives an idea of the vast extent of this marvel of prehistoric engineering. It covers an area of 120 acres, with an average width of 1,500 feet and length of 3,000 feet. The inner circumference is about 1½ miles round, and it has been estimated, as mentioned earlier, that it would require 250,000 men to defend it! It is hard therefore to believe that this construction was originally intended to be a defensive position.

A great puzzle to archaeologists has always been the multiple and labyrinthine east and west entrances at each end of the enclosure, on the left and right sides of the photograph. Originally they may have been built as a

way for processional entry by people of the Neolithic era. Later, when warriors of the Iron Age were using the site as a fortress they probably found them useful as a means of confusing an attacking force trying to gain entry. The fact that so many of these 'hillforts' have two entrances – one north of east and the other south of west – also suggests some form of Sun ceremonial.

Maiden Castle changed hands at different times until the Romans took it over in A.D. 44. After A.D. 367 they built a temple within the enclosure (the small white square within the upper righthand section of the enclosure). At the top of this photograph can be seen a round barrow, which is considered a very fine example.

J. Allan Cash

'. . . a solitude that frightened one a little because it was so vast and calm. The very wind lost its way in it and tried to hide away in the turf. A solitude bounded only by the inner cirque of the horizon, and beyond that the "flaming ramparts of the world", and beyond that the plunge into the infinite of solitude.'

H. J. Massingham in *Downland Man*

From the topmost ridge of Maiden Castle, the earth bank sweeps down to the bottom of the fosse, 60 feet below. The way in which the earth banks of all these prehistoric castles follow the line and contours of the hills readily suggests that they were built to strengthen and enhance the flow of natural forces which could flow across the land bearing a beneficent influence.

Ancient Buildings
and other
Stone Structures

Prehistoric man did not spend all his time building mysterious edifices like Stonehenge or Avebury, or constructing huge mounds in which to bury his dead. He also directed his talents and energies towards building homes for his family and livestock, and that these were often well built is shown by the fact that many traces, often reconstructable, of prehistoric huts and even villages have survived up to the present day. Villages such as Chysauster (Cornwall), Skara Brae (Orkney) and Jarlshof (Shetland) have been restored; roofless huts can be seen at sites such as the Iron Age hillfort of Tre'r Ceiri (Caernarvonshire) and Cytiau Gwyddelod, Holyhead Island (Anglesey), and vestiges of hut circles are visible in many places, such as Grimspound (Devon) and Caer Drewyn (Merionethshire).

Underground chambers called fogous or souterrains are often found within the enclosures of ancient villages in the western part of Britain, especially in Ireland, and there is much speculation regarding their purpose. Food storage or places of refuge are the most widely accepted answers; but we should not dismiss the possibility of there being some religious or spiritual reason for their construction. It is thought that the sacred mysteries of antiquity were of a psychic nature, introducing the initiate to the invisible world by means of a state of heightened consciousness which temporarily enabled the spirit of the initiate to experience physical death and the state of future being. These mysteries were said to be enacted in underground chambers from which all light was excluded. Fogous and souterrains could have been built in order to focus the earth's subtle energies into the chamber and its occupants, and this factor may have been considered during the planning of churches, cathedrals and other religious buildings in later centuries. The Hopi Indians who lived in north Arizona, USA, even today perform their secret ceremonies, when they commune with their gods, in underground chambers known as kivas. These are entered from the surface by vertical ladders.

Recent experiments in caves and potholes seem to suggest that conditions for ESP and telepathy are made more favourable by one or both participants in an experiment being underground. An article on this subject in the *Journal of Paraphysics* (Vol. 4 No. 5 1970) finished with the following paragraph:

'The fascination of caves and potholes lends itself to facile psychological interpretation (as do many facets of existence) such as "desire to return to the womb" or simply plain escapism; the three-dimensional underground pre-historic mazes called "weems" built by the ancient Picts in N. Scotland (as at Smoo Cave) shows that this subconscious urge is not of recent origin; and it is natural to speculate whether this bears any relationship to the euphoria claimed to be experienced by Eileen Garrett in her Faraday Cage experiments (see Vol. 1, No. 5, for a fuller report). It may well be that the wet earth surrounding caverns dampens electro-magnetic radiation (with which the brain is normally bombarded) thus giving the percipient a chance to perceive other types of radiation, possibly transdimensional.'

An example of a weem is Pitcur earth house in Angus, Scotland. It is 200 feet long, 6 feet deep and 3 feet wide, and lined with large stone slabs. As the name 'earth house' reveals, these constructions are gener-ally considered to have been winter dwelling-places for the peasants, but that need not be the only interpretation of such strange, under-ground constructions. *Weem* is close to *wamha* meaning 'cave', and *wame* meaning 'womb', both words of lowland Scotland; and the old English for 'womb' was *wambe*.

Similar to fogous, souterrains and weems are the Kentish dene-holes and labyrinths of caverns. At Chislehurst is a honeycomb of caves, of which it has been said, 'There is an air of profound mystery pervading the place: a hundred indications suggest that it was a subterranean Stonehenge; and one is struck with a sense of wonder, and even of awe, as the dim lamplight reveals the extraordinary works which surround us.' Dene-holes are conventionally thought to have been formed simply as lime or chalk quarries, but their regular shape (a central shaft from which open six chambers, rather like the petals round the centre of a flower) suggests that other purposes were behind their construction. Could these holes have helped ascetics to obtain their mystical experi-ences, as has been suggested for fogous and souterrains? Perhaps individual holes and caves were the dwelling-places of early hermits, and the clusters were the earliest monasteries. At Margate, the Snake grotto is decorated with a shellwork mosaic, and may have been an early shrine.

If we believe the suggestion that in olden times a cave symbolized the womb, and that this might partly explain the preference of early man to bury his dead in an earth-covered chamber, it is only a natural extension of this belief to suggest that certain races of men were troglodytes and lived and worshipped in underground holes and caves. Is it possible that if early man had heightened powers of sensitivity and a well developed level of telepathic ability, many of these underground chambers, whose purpose is a mystery to us and which were used by later races as tombs, might have been what we would now call communication centres? Perhaps they not only enabled an instant means of communication throughout the world, but also on an interplanetary and intergalactic level, not to mention the interdimensional possibilities.

Like the fogous, souterrains, weems and dene-holes, a certain amount of mystery and speculation still surround the stone towers called brochs in Scotland, and those called round towers in Ireland. Twentieth century archaeologists have interpreted these structures in the light of present-day conventions and beliefs, possibly forgetting that ways of life and thought were very different in the centuries long past. Their interpretations may be and probably partly are true, but we should never forget that pronouncements perhaps a thousand years later, however scholarly they sound, stand very little chance of being completely accurate. There is still room for speculation by lively minds – so long as the evidence is not distorted. So among the material on brochs and round towers which follows, all interpretations of these structures will be given, so that the reader can make his own decisions on the strength of the ideas presented.

Other items appearing in this section illustrate other aspects of early man's constructional efforts, including the building of bridges and the digging of mines, though it should also be realized that the activity illustrated took place during a period of around three thousand years from 2000 B.C. to A.D. 1000 and therefore represents many generations of man's existence.

Mousa broch is the best-preserved example of a type of building which is peculiar to Scotland. There are ninety-five brochs in Shetland, over 100 in Orkney, and over 500 throughout Scotland, mostly in the north. They were usually built by the sea or on exposed land, with good agricultural land close by, and are thought by most people to have been fortified farmsteads, protecting the inhabitants against frequent raiders. Mainly built in the Iron Age, though some have revealed Stone Age remains, none were constructed after the second century A.D.

A typical groundplan of a broch shows spokes (passages with chambers at the ends) radiating outwards from a central chamber. In some quarters brochs are known as peels, and at Peel Castle on the Isle of Man is the legendary grave 30 yards long of the first king of Eubonia (the ancient name for the island), who was three-legged. The three legs appear arranged like the spokes of a wheel in the arms of the island. Other similarities to this and to the broch groundplan are the swastika (see Carew cross in 'Archaic crosses and carvings') and the solar wheeled cross (see the illustration of the doorway of St Fechan's church, Fore, in 'The sanctity of ancient sites'). In legend, especially in the outer isles, the fairies are associated with the brochs.

broch on Mousa Island, Shetland   HU 457236 (4)

This broch now stands over 40 feet high, taller than most other brochs, and has been restored at various times. The only opening in the thick external wall is the doorway, and inside a passage leads to a central chamber. All round the walls, right to the top of the broch, are small chambers, and a stairway winds gradually to the top of the building.

'The question of the Origin and Uses of the Round Towers of Ireland has so frequently occupied the attention of distinguished modern antiquaries, without any decisive result, that it is now generally considered as beyond the reach of conclusive investigation;' – thus George Petrie, R.H.A., V.P.R.I.A., begins his book published in 1845, *The Ecclesiastical Architecture of Ireland, Anterior to the Anglo-Norman Invasion; Comprising an Essay on the Origin and Uses of the Round Towers of Ireland, Which Obtained the Gold Medal and Prize of the Royal Irish Academy*. (They don't write titles like that any more.)

The author later states that he believes the round towers to be of Christian and ecclesiastical origin, erected between the fifth and thirteenth centuries. Their purpose was to serve as belfries and for storing sacred utensils, books, relics, etc.; and also to act as places of refuge for the priests during times of trouble. A secondary use was as beacons and watch-towers, whenever the necessity arose.

However, other suggestions have been made concerning their origin and use. Both Danish and Phoenician origins have been suggested, and the following uses: fire-temples; places from which to proclaim the Druidical festivals; gnomons or astronomical observatories; phallic emblems; Buddhist temples; anchorite towers, or stylite columns; penitential prisons; belfries; keeps, or monastic castles; beacons and watch-towers.

Round towers are, except for a few examples in Scotland, peculiar to Ireland, where almost a hundred remain standing today. Several are illustrated in this section.

round tower on
Devenish Island, Lower
Lough Erne, Co.
Fermanagh   H 225470
(N.I. 1″ map 4; Eire ½″
map 3)

This round tower stands
81 feet tall within a
monastic site on a small
island. Close by are the
remains of three churches,
several cross-slabs and a
mediaeval sculptured
cross.

wall near Tintagel,
Cornwall
SX 073863 (185)

Stone walls of herringbone
design are quite often seen
in the Boscastle/Tintagel
area, and it has been
suggested that they show
Cretan influence, this
design being common in
the walls on the island
of Crete.

Janet Bord

Reece Winstone

Tarr Steps, Exmoor,
Somerset
SS 868321 (164)

This prehistoric bridge,
possibly dating originally
from around 1000 B.C.,
crosses the river Barle
near Winsford. Some of
the stones weigh 5 tons,
and legend tells how they
were placed there by the
Devil in one night in order
to win a wager from
another giant who was
challenging his power;
the steps are also called
the Devil's Bridge.

the Great Belfry, round tower at Clonmacnoise, near
Athlone, Co. Offaly   N 010306 (Eire ½″ map 15)

A monastery was founded at Clonmacnoise in A.D. 548–9,
and in the following centuries it was a great centre of
learning. Now the site holds a cathedral, several churches,
crosses, grave slabs, and two round towers. The round
tower shown here is said to have been built by Fergal
O'Rourke who died in 964, and it was restored after having
been struck by lightning in 1134, so that the present
structure is largely twelfth century.

Grimes Graves, near Brandon, Norfolk
TL 816898 (136)

In a 34-acre clearing surrounded by pine trees have been found 346 shafts into these important flint mines. Two shafts have been reopened, and can now be visited. Antler picks which were used as mining tools were discovered in the mines, together with an altar of flints round which were placed antlers, a chalk lamp and balls, a carving of a pregnant woman, and a phallus. The active working of these mines has been dated to 2500–1700 B.C.; flint knapping is still carried on today at nearby Brandon.

Chysauster village, near Madron, Cornwall
SW 473350 (189)

This a fine example of a prehistoric village, thought to have
been occupied from the second century B.C. to the third
century A.D. The remains of eight courtyard houses, lying
along a street, can be seen, also a ruined fogou and terraced
garden plots. In the foreground of the picture is a posthole
for the post which held up the roof.

fogou at Carn Euny, Sancreed, Cornwall
SW 403288 (189)

A fogou is a low passage, usually underground, walled and
roofed with large stones, frequently found close by an old
dwelling site. Their purpose is not known for certain, but the
most popular explanations are storage chambers for food, or
hideaways. Cornish fogous are similar to those of north-west
France, where they are called souterrains, as they are in
Ireland and east and north-east Scotland, where they are
also found.

   The fogou pictured here (looking from the inside towards
the main entrance) is in the village of Carn Euny which dates
from the first century B.C. An unusual feature of this fine
fogou, 66 feet long, is a circular side chamber which once had
a corbelled roof.

Drumena souterrain, Mourne Mountains, Co. Down   J 311340

Referring to Co. Down, Borlase said: 'All this part of Ireland abounds with Caves not only under mounts, forts, and castles, but under plain fields, some winding into little hills and risings like a volute or ram's horn, others run in zigzag like a serpent; others again right forward connecting cell with cell.'

There are many thousands of souterrains in Ireland, and they are thought to be generally more recent than those of Brittany or elsewhere in Britain, dating from the early Christian period or later. Usages were mainly for food storage and refuge, and more recently smuggled goods and firearms have been hidden in them! The souterrain at Drumena, whose entrance is shown here, is 50 feet long and 7 feet high, and is situated in a cashel, or drystone 'fort'.

Bearing in mind the evidence from other parts of Britain which suggests the one-time existence of troglodyte communities, perhaps the Irish tunnels were of earlier date than is generally supposed, and were the subterranean dwellings of a race, perhaps the mysterious Tuatha de Danaan, or children of Dan, who were popularly reputed to live underground.

Din Lligwy, near Llanalgo, Anglesey   SH 496862 (106)

Here are the massive stone remains of an ancient village, with round and squarish stone buildings within an enclosing wall. This particular type of homestead is peculiar to north-west Wales.

Clochan-na-Carraige, in Kilmurvy townland, Inishmore, Aran Islands, Co. Galway   L 822116 (Eire $\frac{1}{2}''$ map 14)

Stone clochans, or beehive huts, are ancient structures (usually Bronze Age) originally used as dwellings, and now, in parts of Ireland and other high rural areas such as Pembrokeshire, used as store-houses. In Ireland, some beehive huts were heated and used as 'sweat houses', on a similar principle to the present-day Turkish bath.

There are many beehive huts in the Irish Aran Islands, but Clochan-na-Carraige is the best preserved. Its internal measurements are 19 feet $\times$ $7\frac{1}{2}$ feet $\times$ 8 feet high, with walls 4 feet thick at the base, and two doors only 3 feet high. The roof has two apertures in the centre, serving the double purpose of window and chimney.

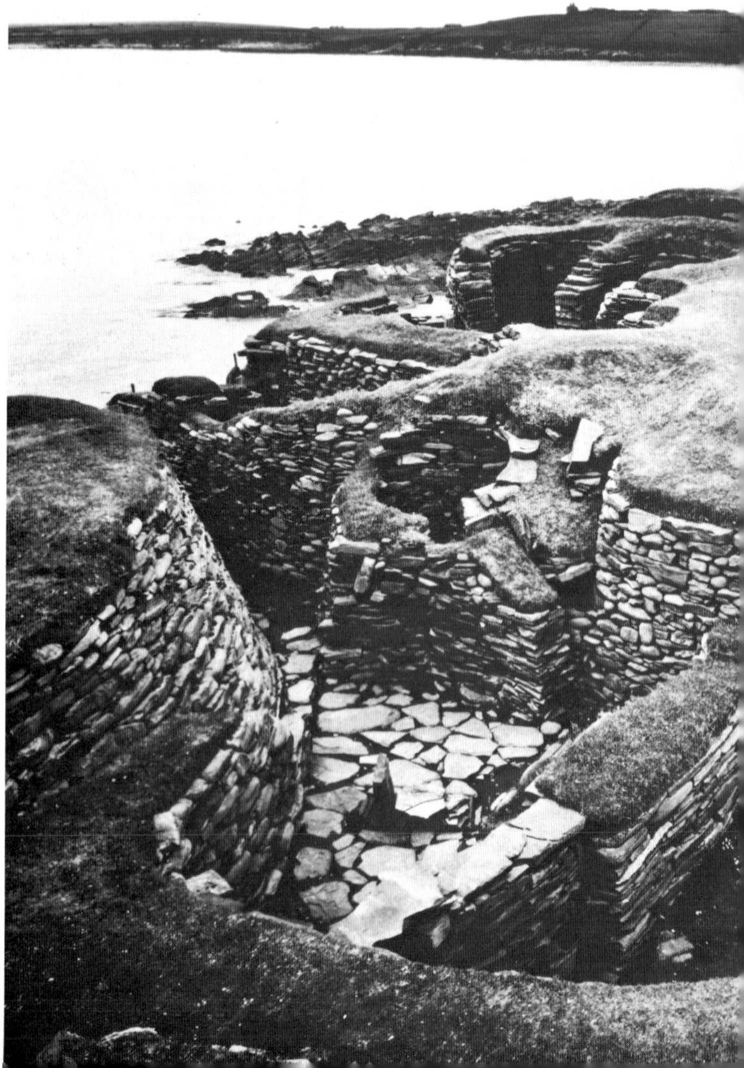

Jarlshof, Sumburgh Head, Shetland   HU 397096 (4)

This early settlement was probably first occupied around
2000 B.C., and was inhabited for 3,000 years. Later peoples
(from the Stone, Bronze and Iron Ages, and Vikings) built
their own houses within the same site, so that today remains
from several different periods can be seen. As at Skara Brae
in the Orkneys, the whole village was buried by sand during
a storm, which explains why it is so well preserved today.

'fire tower' at Brechin, Angus   NO 596601 (43)

The influence of the Irish round towers can be seen in this
100 foot high tower at Brechin in Scotland. Dated between
A.D. 990 and 1012, it adjoins the ancient cathedral, unlike the
Irish towers which stand apart from the churches. A door
leads from inside the tower to the interior of the cathedral,
but no other door opens from the tower.

The Sanctity
of Ancient Sites

The changeover in religious allegiance from decadent paganism to
Christianity took place during the Romanization of Britain, but it was
by no means an immediate or clearcut change. Christianity was pro-
claimed the official religion of Britain early in the fourth century A.D.
a hundred years before the Romans left, but it was many years before
the hold of the Christian Church over the people was as strong as its
proponents desired, and in fact it could be said that all traces of paganism have not been completely wiped out to this day! (See 'The rites of
spring and other pagan ceremonies'.) That the British people were still
practising their old religions in the eleventh century can be seen from a
law passed by King Canute: 'We earnestly forbid every heathenism:
heathenism is that men worship idols; that is, that they worship heathen
gods, and the sun or moon, fire or rivers, water-wells or stones, or
forest trees of any kind, or love witchcraft or promote morthwork
[morth = Norman word for secret killings] of any wise.'

The first missionaries of Christianity must have found the devotion
to the old religions stronger and more difficult to eradicate than they
had expected, because there is much evidence that they had to make
compromises which often involved absorbing old rites and beliefs into
the new religion. The pagan gods and goddesses were canonized as
Christian saints – Brid became St Bridget, St Brigit or St Bride, Ma
and Matrona became Mary, Santan, the Holy Fire, became St Anne,
Sinclair, the Holy Light, became St Clare – and there is doubt as to the
origins of other saints, such as St Gulval and St Wol. An interesting
discovery that goes a long way towards confirming the resilience of
paganism is that many Christian churches which were founded in the
early centuries were built upon pagan sacred sites. This emphasizes the
tremendous sanctity of these sites, and that people were very loth to
desert them.

In A.D. 601 Pope Gregory, in a letter to Abbot Mellitus who was
about to visit England, stated the action to be taken in order to wean
the British from paganism to Christianity.

This was written 300 years after the country was officially termed
'Christian'.

'When (by God's help) you come to our most reverend brother, Bishop Augustine, I want you to tell him how earnestly I have been pondering over the affairs of the English: I have come to the conclusion that the temples of the idols in England should not on any account be destroyed. Augustine must smash the idols, but the temples themselves should be sprinkled with holy water and altars set up in them in which relics are to be enclosed. For we ought to take advantage of well-built temples by purifying them from devil-worship and dedicating them to the service of the true God. In this way, I hope the people (seeing their temples are not destroyed) will leave their idolatry and yet continue to frequent the places as formerly, so coming to know and revere the true God.'

Churches everywhere figure in siting legends, many of which tell how at night, during the building of the new church, the Devil secretly moved the stones to a new site, often on a hilltop. This could be folk-lore's way of telling how the Christians had to build the churches where the recently converted pagans wanted them, on holy sites which meant so much to them and which were usually on sacred hills or mounds. Although reconstruction of graveyards has changed the origi-nal shapes of many of them over the centuries, there are still churches to be found which definitely stand on circular mounds within tell-tale circular graveyards, and in many cases the sites were originally pre-Christian burial mounds and meeting places.

Some churches have even more outstanding markers proving the antiquity of the site. In the churchyard of Rudston church in Yorkshire stands a giant monolith, over 25 feet high and 6 feet wide (see illustra-tion in this section); Corwen church in Merionethshire has an ancient stone 6 feet long embedded in its east wall; there is a carving of a figure, identified very tentatively as a Celtic god, on a stone slab set into an outside wall of Copgrove church, Yorkshire; and the font in Old Radnor church, Wales, is shaped from a megalithic stone.

It is not only churches which are built on sacred sites, for other religious buildings, such as cathedrals, chapels, monasteries, abbeys and priories, were also founded at places of special importance. Many religious buildings, especially cathedrals, were up until quite recent times designed and built by craftsmen who imbued their creations with a magnificent glory which was greatly enhanced by the spiritual atmos-phere associated with the site. The shapes and proportions incorpor-ated into such sacred structures were important in helping to maintain the spirituality of the site by drawing down the cosmic energies into the building.

Some castles are also found to have been built upon ancient sites, usually high places, but whether this was anything to do with the sanctity of the site, or the fact that a hill, natural or man-made, provided the beginnings of a defensive construction, is not so clear; probably the latter, especially when the castle was built after the eleventh century. The early 'castles' were earthworks rather than the solid buildings we associate with the word today, and these, together with the Norman motte and 'bailey', very often made use of ancient mounds as the foundation for their defences. Many such sites are far older in their origins than is generally realized, and were in the first place conceived as sacred mounds.

Ben Darby

'The Cathedral of the South Downs', Alfriston, Sussex
TQ 522030 (183)

A supernatural agency is credited with choosing the site for
this church. The stones were moved each night from the
original site, and placed in a field. Then one day at dawn, a
man saw four oxen lying together in the field, with their
bodies forming the shape of a Greek cross, and this was
taken to be a sign that the church should be built on that
spot. It actually stands on a circular mound, as can be seen in
this photograph taken at dawn, and this tends to confirm the
early sanctity of the site which is echoed in the legend.

118

inscribed stone, Gallarus, Co. Kerry
Q 355049 (Eire ½″ map 20)

This 4 foot stone stands close by Gallarus oratory.
The inscription, in Graeco-Roman or Byzantine
characters of the fourth or fifth centuries, reads THE
STONE OF COLUM SON OF . . . MEL. It also
carries a wheeled cross; in the East in ancient times,
and also in early Northern mythology, this was a Sun
symbol.

Gallarus oratory, near Ballyferriter, Co. Kerry
Q 355049 (Eire ½″ map 20)

These stone oratories, of which there are several in
Ireland, are thought to have been very early Christian
churches. This one at Gallarus, possibly dating from
the eighth century, is the best-preserved example to
be seen today, and may well be the oldest church in
Ireland. The walls are of dry stone and 3½ feet thick,
sloping towards the top so that the whole building
looks like an upturned boat. This shape may have a
special purpose – to attract and concentrate the
cosmic energies along the roof ridge, and then
disperse them within the building, to the spiritual
and physical benefit of anyone engaged in religious
activity inside.

Wales Tourist Board

Tintern Abbey, Monmouthshire   SO 533000 (155)

'*The Abbey of Tinterne is the most beautiful and
picturesque of all our gothic monuments : there every
arch infuses a solemn energy, as it were, into
inanimate nature, a sublime antiquity breathes
mildly in the heart ; and the soul, pure and
passionless, appears susceptible of that state of
tranquillity, which is the perfection of every earthly
wish.*'

Bucke's *Beauties, Harmonies,
and Sublimities of Nature*

The ruins of this abbey, founded by the Cistercians in 1131,
stand in a quiet and beautiful rural setting by the river Wye.

120

Pictor

St Michael's church, Brentor, Dartmoor, Devon   SX 471804 (187)

One of the more familiar legends connected with the siting of churches is told of this church on Brentor. It was originally planned to build it at the foot of the hill, but the stones were secretly and mysteriously moved to the top of the hill. So the builders finally gave in and built the church on the high point. Note also that this church is dedicated to St Michael, whose name is frequently found at churches built on hilltops or pre-Christian mounds. Another interesting fact is that several leys pass through this site. (For information about leys, see 'Trackways and leys – the unseen power'.)

Edinburgh Castle   NT 252736 (62)

Dominating the Scottish city of Edinburgh is the Castle, built on an outcrop of rock which may previously have held an Iron Age hillfort. The oldest part of the castle is the tiny St Margaret's chapel, dating from the beginning of the twelfth century.

Scottish Tourist Board

Glendalough, Co. Wicklow   T 126968 (Eire ½″ map 16)

One of the most famous religious centres in early Christian Ireland, the monastery at Glendalough was founded by St Kevin in the sixth century. However, the site appears to have been of significance long before that, for close by one of the lakes in the 'Glen of the Two Lakes' is St Kevin's Bed. This is an artificial cave thought to be a rock-cut tomb dating from around 2000 B.C. (See the Dwarfie Stane in 'The standing stones and circles of prehistory' for a similar construction.) The site covers a mile and a half in the valley, and there are the ruins of churches, crosses, a stone fort, a cathedral, and a 100 foot tall round tower to be seen.

St Saviour's Priory, Glendalough, Co. Wicklow   T 126968 (approx.) (Eire ½″ map 16)

Much Romanesque decoration graces this twelfth century church, and the drawing shows the chancel archway as it was before reconstruction took place at the end of the nineteenth century.

Old Sarum, near Salisbury, Wiltshire   SU 137327 (167)

The original earthwork which was developed and altered in later years is generally thought to have dated from the Iron Age, but it may well be much earlier. The mound in the centre was built in Norman times, and held a castle. The foundations of the old cathedral can still be seen; this was built in 1078 but soon replaced by a new cathedral at Salisbury (New Sarum), $1\frac{1}{2}$ miles away.

Old Sarum is a good example of an ancient site which retained its importance through many centuries. This great earthwork and the town which had grown up upon it were probably abandoned during the fifteenth century. (See also 'Trackways and leys – the unseen power'.)

Noel Habgood

Salisbury Cathedral and the River Avon, Wiltshire   SU 143295 (167)

This cathedral replaces the one originally standing at Old Sarum, which was abandoned early in the thirteenth century, ostensibly because of the general unsuitability of the site. The real reason may be deeper than that, and connected with the changing sacred power of the sites. Both sites are on a clearly defined ley which is illustrated in 'Trackways and leys – the unseen power', later in the book.

While searching for a new site for the cathedral, Bishop Richard Poore had a vision of the Virgin, who told him where to build, and so the new cathedral at New Sarum, or Salisbury, was started in 1220. It is, except for the spire and part of the tower, entirely Early English Gothic, and its beauty must be seen to be fully appreciated. The spire, the tallest in England, was added in 1334. Richly carved stones from the cathedral at Old Sarum were built into the close wall.

St Illtud's church, Caldey Island, Pembrokeshire   SS 141962 (152)

A monastic community was first established on the island in the sixth century, and although there are no remains of the Celtic monastery, its site is thought to have been where St Illtud's church and the monastic buildings now stand. These buildings date from the thirteenth and fourteenth centuries; the church with its 50 foot tower is to the right of the picture, the monastic buildings to the left. The unusual looking spire is now 40 inches out of the perpendicular. The oldest part of the church is the sanctuary, paved with large black pebbles from the beach. Also inside the church are an Ogham stone (for an illustration of this, see 'Archaic crosses and carvings') and a recent stained glass window showing St Illtud in his youth as a knight of King Arthur's court. The church is still in use, but between the Reformation and 1900 was used for various non-ecclesiastical purposes, including a laundry and a brewery. It now stands in the monastery farmyard.

Castell Coch, near Cardiff, Glamorgan, before restoration in 1875 ST 131826 (154)

This thirteenth century castle, built on the summit of a steep cliff, appears to be on the site of older fortifications. An underground passage is said to lead from the castle to Cardiff, and this may indicate the presence of a ley, as may the fact that this hill was once a beacon site. (For information on leys, see 'Trackways and leys – the unseen power'.)

Rudston monolith, near Bridlington, Yorkshire
TA 097677 (93)

This gigantic stone, the tallest standing stone in Britain,
rears up from among the graves close by the church at
Rudston. The church is Norman, but the stone dates back to
1600–1000 B.C. It is 25½ feet high (above ground), 6 feet
wide and 2¼ feet thick, weighing about 40 tons, and there is
said to be as much below ground as above.

This stone presumably marked a sacred site before the
church was built, and, unlike most places where the
markstone has disappeared, this one would have been too
much trouble to uproot, and so was left standing. (For
information on markstones, see 'Trackways and leys – the
unseen power'.) Legend attributes its placing to the Devil,
who flung it at the church but was once again thwarted by
poor marksmanship.

One wonders what must have been the reactions through
the centuries of the various incumbents at having such an
obvious and obtrusive phallic symbol permanently on view
outside their church.

128

Janet Bord

St Michael's Mount, near Marazion, Cornwall SW 515298 (189)

St Michael's Mount is a fabled and holy place; Celtic saints are said to have
dwelt there, and a hermit once saw St Michael in a vision. It is a part of the
lost and legendary land of Lyonesse, submerged in some great catastrophe of
the distant past. One of the legends of the Mount harks back to the days
when Mount's Bay, between Penzance and Marazion, was dry land covered
with thick forest where lived giant Cormoran and his wife Cormelian.

  They were building a stronghold of white granite from neighbouring hills,
which they carried in their aprons. One day, while Cormelian was working
hard, she noticed that Cormoran was sleeping, so she decided to fetch
greenstone rock instead, because the journey would be shorter. But
Cormoran awoke before she could unload the rock. He kicked her, her apron
string broke, and the rock fell to the ground. Today, by the causeway
leading to the Mount, is a solitary rock of greenstone known as Chapel Rock,
and part of it can be seen to the right of the photograph. Why was the white
granite so important? White stones feature at other ancient sites, for
example at Newgrange in Ireland where pieces of white quartz originally
covered the mound.

St David's Cathedral, Pembrokeshire
SM 752254 (138/151)

Sheltering in a hollow, this powerful building is best seen on
a wet day, when the rain brings out the rich colours of the
exterior stonework. The present building is mainly twelfth
century, though a cathedral was founded at St David's much
earlier, probably in the early sixth century.

Colin Bord

Lilbourne, Northamptonshire SP 561775 (132)

Lilbourne is one of the many places throughout Britain
where the old village church, in this case All Saints dating
back at least to the thirteenth century, stands very close to an
ancient earthwork. This again indicates that the churches
were built as close as possible to the sacred pagan sites.

Lilbourne was the site of the Roman settlement
Tripontium; the earthwork, probably pre-Roman, is close
to the River Avon, the water from which was used to flood the
ditches beneath the banks.

The Abbey, Glastonbury, Somerset, as it was early in
the twentieth century   ST 501387 (165)

*'The stones of the Abbey are overthrown, but its spirit lives on
like a haunting presence, and many have seen its ghost.
Dreaming alone in the quiet of the great roofless church, the
ghostly pillars re-form themselves to the inward eye ; the high
altar shines with its lights and a chanting draws near down the
hollow aisles.'*

Dion Fortune in *Avalon of the Heart*

According to legend, Joseph of Arimathea sailed to England
as a missionary, and came to Avalon, the Isle of Apples.
Reaching Wearyall Hill near Glastonbury, he stuck his staff
into the ground, and from it grew a thorn bush. The holy
thorn in the Abbey grounds, which flowers in mid-winter,
is said to be a cutting from Joseph's original thorn.

The present ruined abbey stands on the spot where the
first wattle church was built at Glastonbury; the first abbey
was founded in A.D. 688. King Arthur is said to have been
buried in the grounds – but for more details of the King
Arthur legends see 'King Arthur and the Quest for the Grail'.

Noel Habgood

The Rock of Cashel, Co. Tipperary   S 073407
(Eire ½″ map 18)

A wealth of early religious buildings covers the summit of a
200 foot high limestone outcrop. This site was chosen to be
a royal seat in pre-Christian times, and was once the
ecclesiastical capital of Munster. A cashel (stone fort) was
built here by the King of Munster in the fifth century; the
oldest building still standing is the Round Tower, 85 feet
high and 51 feet in circumference, which is probably tenth
century. Behind the tower are Cormac's Chapel, a thirteenth
century cathedral, and the hall of the Vicar's Choral, dating
from the fifteenth century and later – all now in ruins. The
High Cross is twelfth century.

   An amusing incident in the history of the Rock took place
during St Patrick's visit there. He converted King Aenghus
to Christianity, and during the baptism, St Patrick
accidentally stuck his crozier into the king's foot. The king
endured the pain without complaint, thinking it was all part
of the ceremony!

134

Cormac's Chapel, Rock of Cashel, Co. Tipperary
S 073407 (Eire ½" map 18)

'The most remarkable Romanesque church in Ireland' was
consecrated in 1134, building having been begun in 1127 at
the instigation of Bishop Cormac MacCarthy. The church
is of architectural interest for several reasons, one being its
steep stone roof, and shows German influence, especially in
the square tower on each side.

Geoffrey N. Wright

Pendragon Castle, Mallerstang, near Kirkby Stephen, Westmorland
SD 779025 (90)

The ruins to be seen today are of a Norman castle, but before that the site is
said to have been occupied by a castle built by Uther Pendragon during the
fifth century. Uther was king of Britain and father of King Arthur. He wished
to fortify his castle, by diverting the River Eden round it to form a moat,
but he was unsuccessful.

A proverb says,

Let Uther Pendragon do what he can,
Eden will run where Eden ran.

Kilpeck church, Herefordshire   SO 445305 (142)

Kilpeck has a long monastic history, and this church was built in the early
twelfth century on the site of an earlier Anglo-Saxon building. It is famed for
its rich and ornate carvings, which have weathered remarkably little during
eight hundred or so years.

The doorway shown here carries a variety of symbolic designs, possibly
embodying pre-Christian ideas. Below the arch is a grape-bearing Tree of
Life; round the arch are birds, mythical beasts, fishes, a phoenix in flames,
a lion with a human face, zodiac signs and dragons devouring each other.
Serpents can be seen on the shafts, with strange human figures on the
left-hand side.

136

Noel Habg

St Govan's Chapel, St Govan's Head, Pembrokeshire
SR 967930 (138/151)

This tiny chapel, measuring only 18 feet by 12 feet, was probably built in the thirteenth century, but the altar (said to be the tomb of St Govan) and a seat cut into the rock wall are much earlier. It is not possible to count correctly the steps leading from the cliff-top through the chapel and down to the sea, so tradition says. There was once a holy well a few yards away from the chapel, but it has been filled in. St Govan's Head is one of the places in the list of those claimed to be the burial place of Sir Gawain, nephew of King Arthur, who was slain by Sir Launcelot.

138

Northern Ireland Tourist Board

ruined churches at Killevy, near
Newry, Co. Armagh   J 041221

The oldest of the two roofless churches
standing together at this ancient
religious site dates from the ninth
century; the other is eleventh century.
At Killevy was founded in the fifth
century one of the most important
nunneries in Ireland.

Gloucester Cathedral and the ruins
of St Oswald's Priory
SO 831187 (143)

Gloucester was an early site of
Christianity, and where the cathedral
now stands, a Christian church stood
1,800 years ago. The present building
dates from Norman times. The priory
ruins, also called St Katherine's Abbey,
are seventh century.

139

Colin Bord

St Michael and All Angels, Winwick,
Northamptonshire   SP 626738 (133)

This church, in an out-of-the-way rural hamlet surprisingly
close to the M1 motorway, stands on what was originally a
circular moot mound, which can still be clearly seen today.
The first Christian church on this site was built in the
thirteenth century. To the left stands an old tithe barn, and
close by is the sixteenth century manor house. It is recorded
that Sir Thomas Malory, author of the famous *Morte
D'Arthur*, was Lord of the Manor of Winwick.

Noel Habgood

Fountains Abbey, near Ripon, Yorkshire   SE 275683 (91)

Founded by Benedictine monks in 1132–3, Fountains Abbey is a well-preserved example of England's former monastic glory. Particularly attractive are the cloisters with their rhythmic, spreading arches.

Eilean Donan Castle, Ross and Cromarty   NG 881258 (26)

This picturesque Scottish castle was built in 1220 on a tiny island where three sea lochs, Duich, Alsh and Long, meet, and access from the mainland is along a narrow causeway. Damaged in 1719 in the Battle of Glen Shiel, the castle was reconstructed in 1932 in its original tower house style.

Artificial islands were sometimes constructed in the middle of lakes where leys crossed because this was thought to be a particularly favourable site for building as a result. Perhaps this ancient edifice is placed upon such an island. (For information on leys, see 'Trackways and leys – the unseen power'.)

Noel Habgood

Colin Bord

144

The White Tower, the central fortress in the Tower of London
TQ 336805 (160)

Built in the eleventh century by William the Conqueror, the White Tower
has since been a fortress, prison and royal palace. The large windows were
added in the seventeenth century, replacing the Norman arrow slits. It is said
that in the thirteenth century the exterior was whitewashed, hence the name
of White Tower, but its ancient Celtic name was Bryn Gwyn (*gwyn* meaning
white in the sense of being pure or holy, and *bryn* being a hill).

This site was chosen by the Conqueror for his fortress because of its
ancient associations and importance to the British. On this archaic holy spot
stood a sacred mound, similar to the toot hills that are still found all over
Britain. But this was one that was closely associated with the ancient line of
British kings, for it is said that buried here were two illustrious prehistoric
monarchs, Brutus, the reputed founder of London, in 1100 B.C., and
Molmutius, the road builder and lawgiver who was interred about 500 B.C.
The mound at this time had no structure on it, though a royal dwelling was
close by. And at a later time, Sir Thomas Malory records in *Morte D'Arthur*
how Queen Guinevere took refuge in the Tower of London to avoid a
marriage with Sir Mordred.

Down within the foundations of this present structure is said to be a well,
150 feet deep, considered by archaeologists to be of Roman construction.
Such stone-lined shafts as this were thought to have been used in many parts
of the world to assist in astronomical observations by cutting out the ambient
glare of moon and stars, and may also have been used by the ancient
priesthood of pre-Christian Britain. This tradition was continued, for the
north-east pinnacle of the White Tower is circular (on left of picture), and
was an observatory until the seventeenth century when the Royal Observatory
was built further down the river at Greenwich.

Over the centuries there has been so much construction and reconstruction
around the area of the Tower that all that remains to be seen of the original
sacred mound is a slight grassy bank on the south side.

Northern Ireland Tourist Board

Bonamargy Friary, near Ballycastle, Co. Antrim
D 125408 (N.I. 1″ map 1; Eire ½″ map 2)

This Franciscan friary, now ruined, was founded around
1500 by Rory MacQuillan, but was damaged by fire a
century later and attacked early in the seventeenth century,
so it was abandoned around 1642. Among the remains of a
church and the living quarters can be seen carvings of heads
and beasts.

Tempull Ceannanach, Inishmaan, Aran Islands,
Co. Galway

'*This little church . . . measures on the inside but sixteen feet six
inches in length, and twelve feet six inches in breadth ; and its
walls, which are three feet in thickness, are built in a style quite
Cyclopean, the stones being throughout of great size, and one of
them not less than eighteen feet in length – which is the entire
external breadth of the church, – and three feet in thickness.*'

George Petrie in *The Ecclesiastical Architecture of Ireland &c.*

148

Northern Ireland Tourist Board

Moyry Castle, near Jonesborough, Co. Armagh
J 058147 (N.I. 1″ map 8; Eire ½″ map 9)

This squat tower, 24 feet square, was built during Lord
Deputy Mountjoy's Campaign of 1600 to guard the Moyra
Pass. It stands on a mound, which may have been an artificial
mound chosen as the castle site because of its extensive
outlook over the surrounding valley.

Durham Cathedral   NZ 276419 (85)

These impressive pillars form part of the cathedral which
was a shrine for the tomb of St Cuthbert who died in 687.
Founded as a cathedral around 997, building was started in
1093 and the Norman part completed by 1133.

Compare the lozenge and chevron designs on these pillars
with those on the stones at Newgrange, illustrated in
'Archaic crosses and carvings'. Is it not possible that there
was a continuous Masonic tradition which extended from
prehistoric times down to the Norman times and continuing
up until the Middle Ages?

A vertical line of lozenge shapes with their points touching
is a symbol of etheric energy, and has been likened to the
double helix of the DNA spiral, a basic carrier for the subtle
life energies. Some occultists also term the symbol of a
lozenge divided by a horizontal bar as a 'dragon's eye',
perhaps another link with the life-giving 'dragon power' to
be found on ley lines and at ley centres. (For information on
leys, see 'Trackways and leys – the unseen power'.)

Brinklow, near Coventry, Warwickshire   SP 438796 (132)

At the edge of Brinklow churchyard the ground rises steeply to form the outside bank of a large and impressive earthwork. On the far side, opposite the church, is a mound crowned with trees.

The church, dating from at least the thirteenth century, though rebuilt in the fifteenth, is dedicated to St John the Baptist, an indication that Midsummer may have been festivally celebrated in the earthwork. (For information on Midsummer celebrations, see 'The rites of spring and other pagan ceremonies'.) The name Ell Lane, given to a road running alongside the earthwork, also suggests Sun worship, for 'ell' has links with the Greek *ele* meaning 'refulgent', and also with Helios, a name for the Sun. The Cabalists understood 'Ell' to mean 'the Most Luminous'.

The Roman road the Foss Way passes through Brinklow, but the earthwork stands firmly in its way, and so at this point the road makes a deviation around it. As this shows that the earthwork predates the Foss Way, could it also indicate that the Roman road was built along the course of a much older ley? (For information on leys, see 'Trackways and leys – the unseen power'.)

The photographs show the tower of Brinklow church, and in front of it the outer bank of earth, as seen from the top of the mound; and the mound itself. The mound may originally have been moated, for there is at the base a depression in which water now collects.

t Bord

Colin Bord

Reece Winstone

'the heavenly stair', Wells Cathedral, Somerset
ST 552459 (165)

These worn and beautiful steps lead from the north transept
of the cathedral up to the Chapter House (to the right of the
photograph), a peaceful room, octagonal in shape and with a
central pillar. There is an interesting carving to be seen on
a corbel above the stairs, depicting a peasant who is
thrusting his staff into the mouth of a dragon.

Wells has been the seat of a bishop since A.D. 909; the
cathedral dates from the late twelfth century.

Inishcaltra, island in Lough Derg, Co. Clare
R 698850 (Eire $\frac{1}{2}''$ map 15)

There are the ruins of four churches on this holy site where
a monastery was founded in the seventh century by St
Caimin. The drawing shows the western doorway and
chancel arch of St Caimin's church which was first erected
in the seventh century, though since then there have been
changes and rebuilding.

Totnes Castle, Devon   SX 800605 (188)

Totnes takes its name from this artificial sacred hill or 'tot' which stands high above the town and affords magnificent views over the surrounding countryside. A castle was built here by William of Normandy in the eleventh century, though the walls and other remains still to be seen are thirteenth century.

'The trees and underwood that now clothe the Tot have almost obliterated the terraced lines of its original contour, similar to those on Silbury, and other mounds of the same character that have not been planted, lines which only the scientific investigations of our own day have shown were drawn with such consummate skill by the ancient astronomers that by using these as sighting lines, the warning star of sunrise could be observed and the times and seasons fixed.'

E. O. Gordon in *Prehistoric London*

solar wheel above the ancient doorway of St Fechan's
church, Fore, near Castlepollard, Westmeath
N 515704 (Eire $\frac{1}{2}''$ map 16)

In the ancient graveyard stand the remains of St Fechan's
church, partly rebuilt. The huge lintel stone over the
doorway weighs over $2\frac{1}{2}$ tons, and legend has it that workmen
were unable to lift this stone into position. Such a feat was
not beyond St Fechan, who used some unknown power
(levitation?) to raise the stone. Other miracles attributed to
him included making a nearby stream run uphill.

Noel Habgood

Whitby Abbey, Yorkshire NZ 904113 (86)

The stark ruins of this abbey stand on a headland above the
coastal town of Whitby. The first abbey, founded by St
Hilda for King Oswy of Northumbria in A.D. 657, was a
centre of learning. That abbey was destroyed by the Danes
in 867, and a new one was founded in 1087 by the
Benedictines. However, the present ruins are thirteenth
century, and were bombed during the last world war.

156

Holy Wells
and their
Healing Powers

Although not often written about, and rarely visited, Britain's holy wells are in great abundance. Today there are over 1,000 throughout England, the same number in Wales, at least 600 in Scotland, and no fewer than 3,000 in Ireland, and there were once probably more than this. Water was sacred in pre-Christian times, and not only wells but rivers, streams, lakes, springs and fountains were revered. Traditions and legends have remained to testify to the sanctity of such sites, and the following, for example, were sacred lakes and now have legends attached to them: the Silent Pool, Albury, Surrey; Lochmaben in Dumfriesshire; Mathern Pill near Chepstow, Monmouthshire; the village pond at Ewelme, Oxfordshire; and the lake at Loughadrine, Co. Cork.

Medicinal properties were attributed to the water in many of the holy wells, and such beliefs may originally have had some factual basis because of the minerals present in the water. At some wells, customs and legends have grown up concerning their use and what is likely to happen if their surroundings are disturbed.

Some of the wells had small chapels or baptistries built over them, and were used by Christian priests to perform baptisms. This is one way in which Christianity absorbed pagan sites into herself (see also 'The sanctity of ancient sites'), and there are several examples of ancient churches standing in close proximity to wells – East Dereham, Bisley, Llandelga, Jesmond, Lichfield, Watchet, Musselburgh, Strathfillan, etc. In some cases, the holy well is actually found within the church.

One custom attached to several holy wells, and of undoubted antiquity, is still practised today. At the Clootie Well on Culloden Moor, near Inverness, on Culloden Sunday early in May, many people drink at the well and make a wish, throwing a coin into the water as a gift to the spirit dwelling there. Then a piece of rag, called a clootie, is tied to a branch of a nearby tree, and the clooties must be left to rot, for bad luck will result if they are removed. It has been suggested that the custom of hanging clooties on trees dates right back to the times when human sacrifices were made, strips being torn from the garments of the victims and hung upon sacred boughs. There is evidence that the custom of hanging rags upon thorn bushes was also practised at sacred sites generally, not just by holy wells, and that it happened in other parts of the world besides Britain.

Two Manx customs illustrate other ways in which holy well or spring water was accredited with special powers. The water from the well at Glencrutchery was used by the farmers' wives at Onchan, who poured a few drops into their churns to help the butter to form quickly; and in Lezayre the fishermen used to throw handfuls of the spring water up into the sky in the direction of the wind they required for their fishing.

The only holy wells 'on the map' today are those which have been popularized as wishing wells, but many more, in a ruined condition and hidden by foliage, are awaiting rediscovery.

Reece Winstone

Dupath Well, Callington, Cornwall   SX 375692 (186)

A small baptistry, built of granite blocks, stands over this
well which was once visited by pilgrims.

St Nun's Well, Pelynt, Cornwall   SX 225563 (186)

This well was also known locally as St Ninnie's Well and Piskies' Well, pins being thrown into it to keep the little people happy, and to obtain their co-operation with the farming.

    A legend tells how one old farmer decided he would like the granite basin into which the water flowed (it can be seen inside the doorway, decorated with circles and crosses) to use as a pig trough, and so he drove his oxcart to the well to fetch it. He fastened the oxen to the basin, and although it would not move for a long time, they slowly began to drag it up the hill to the cart. 'Here, however, it burst away from the chains which held it, and, rolling back again to the well, made a sharp turn and regained its old position, where it has remained ever since. Nor will anyone again attempt its removal, seeing that the farmer, who was previously well-to-do in the world, never prospered from that day forward. Some people say, indeed, that retribution overtook him on the spot, the oxen falling dead, and the owner being struck lame and speechless.' (*The Legendary Lore of the Holy Wells of England* by Robert Charles Hope).

St Hilda's Well, Hinderwell, Yorkshire
NZ 791170 (approx.) (86)

Tradition tells how the monks journeying between Whitby
Abbey and Kirkham Abbey used to make this well one of
their resting-places.

AMBREWS.WELL

Reece Winstone

St Senan's Well, Dunass, Co. Clare

'At Dunass, county Clare, is a well noted for many healing virtues from having been blessed by St Senan, who also left the impress of his knees on a flat rock near the brink. The country people kneel in these indentations as they stoop to drink, and find relief as they touch the impression left by the saint. The well presents nothing peculiar to distinguish it from a thousand other springs of the same kind, save the characteristic votive offerings made at it. These chiefly consist of wooden bowls, whole and fractured teacups, blacking-pots, and similar singular thank-offerings to the Patron Saint of the parish.'

W. G. Wood-Martin in *Traces of the Elder Faiths of Ireland*

St Ambrew's Well, Crantock, near Newquay,
Cornwall   SW 790604 (approx.) (185)

This old carved doorway protects one of Cornwall's many ancient holy wells. St Ambrew's Well is reputed to be over a thousand years old, and can be found in one of the village lanes.

Hill Figures:
Signals
to the Gods?

In several parts of Britain, white horses and other figures can be seen on the hill-slopes. These were formed by cutting away the top surface and exposing the stark white chalk a few inches below. From the earliest times until the present day, men seem to have been fascinated by the opportunity to make a landmark that can be seen for miles around – but the best vantage point for most of these figures is from the air. . . .

The oldest figure is the strange horse at Uffington, and the most recent are regimental badges cut earlier in this century. The latter do not concern us here. The age of the Uffington 'horse' (doesn't it look more like a dragon?) is acknowledged to be very great. Just how old it is nobody knows, but the 'educated guesses' of the archaeologists place it at 100 B.C.

The other horses, of which there are several throughout the country, are said to be eighteenth and nineteenth century as there are various records and memories of them being cut then. It could well be that these were figures being recut (and modernized) or cleaned (known as scouring), and were in fact of an age comparable to the Uffington horse. Until the eighteenth century they were largely unknown and completely ignored. It is on record that the original horse at Westbury, which by all accounts was as strange a shape as the Uffington figure, was destroyed in 1778 and recut on conventional lines by a local character who considered himself to be a judge of horseflesh; while the Broad Town horse in Wiltshire, which was claimed to have been cut by a local farmer in 1864, was later found to have existed at the beginning of that century. Probably more than one childish memory of a scouring has been turned by time into a spurious record of a cutting.

The Uffington horse was dated as Iron Age because a similar figure appears on coins of that time. But is there any reason why the Belgae should not have used on their coinage a figure of great antiquity and veneration, as we do with Britannia who, until recently, appeared on our coins and still does on our banknotes? Some authorities believe that this ancient goddess came from the eastern Mediterranean with Brut, who built his new city on the site which is now London.

164

Although they are in the majority, horses (or dragons) are not the only ancient hill figures. The Cerne Abbas giant and the Long Man of Wilmington are two human representations, and other lesser-known figures have been re-excavated in recent years. Whiteleaf Cross near Princes Risborough, Buckinghamshire, may originally have been an astrological or phallic symbol later reshaped into a cross. Another possible phallic symbol is Watlington White Mark, Oxfordshire. There is no doubt that many more figures await rediscovery (if this is possible now that the landscape has been so altered), and two more giants are on record, lying hidden at Plymouth Hoe and Shotover Hill near Oxford.

Although the known hill figures are usually white because of the underlying chalk, another horse was the Red Horse of Tysoe, near Banbury, Warwickshire. He cannot be seen today, but did exist at one time. The colour was because of the red soil at the site, and the horse may have been cut in 1461 to commemorate the Earl of Warwick's horse, killed in battle. It could, however, have been cut before this, and later scoured in remembrance of the Earl's horse.

While searching for the lost horse of Tysoe in 1963, S. G. Wildman discovered not a horse, but a whole collection of other figures. Probing for their outlines, he made out what appeared to be a human figure wielding a whip or piece of rope, a bird, perhaps a goose, with its head pointing upwards, and behind them an unidentifiable animal possibly a horse, dragon or Sun Lion. Below all these was the vague outline of perhaps another animal. This animal is around 300 feet long, and the height of the man is 160 feet. The figures, which were not excavated, could be discerned by most people on oblique aerial photographs, but not on vertical ones.

Mr Wildman links his human figure with the Saxon god Tiw (Tysoe = Tiw's hillspur), who is connected with a story of the binding of an evil beast, i.e. a victory over the powers of darkness, or the victory of spring over winter (Spring Hill and Sunrising Hill are close by). The full story of the rediscovery of the Tysoe figures, together with details of their exact location, can be read in *The Black Horsemen* by S. G. Wildman.

Mr Wildman did in fact find an old horse, but this was on another occasion, and it was carved on rock at Bidston Hill, Cheshire. This may have connections with those horses cut out of the hillsides, and more information on the Bidston Hill horse can be found in 'Archaic crosses and carvings'.

A curious factor which has more than a passing significance is the number of sites where an earthwork is found on the hilltop above a chalk-cut figure. That these hillforts were in fact defensive positions is open to doubt (see 'Earthworks on the hilltops'). A possibility that appears not to have been considered by conventional archaeology is that they were the sacred enclosures wherein rites connected with the fertility of man, beast and earth were enacted. These ancient rituals of song and dance have been transmitted through the ages, becoming more and more garbled in form, until the last century, when they were celebrated as fairs and games and since then have mostly died out completely. (See 'The rites of spring and other pagan ceremonies'.)

Legends and festivities involving horses may point back to ancient horse worship, and therefore link up with the hillside horses. Coventry's famous legendary character Lady Godiva, who rides, naked but modestly covered by her long hair, on a white horse through the town, may be one example, for Harold Bayley in *Archaic England* links her with Good Hipha, *hipha* being the Tyrian title of the Great Mother whose name also meant 'mare'. The old nursery rhyme 'Ride a cock horse to Banbury Cross, See a fine lady upon a white horse. Rings on her fingers and bells on her toes, She shall have music wherever she goes' may also be a memory of a similar festivity. And what about ghostly white horses, reputedly seen at various places, e.g. Finchampstead, Berkshire?

Aerofilms

Cerne Abbas giant, on Giant Hill near Cerne Abbas,
Dorset   ST 667016 (178)

The Cerne Abbas giant is now thought of as a fertility
symbol, and he has long been associated with fertility.
Above him on the hilltop can be seen the enclosure where
maypole celebrations have been held for centuries (May
Day has strong connexions with fertility ceremonies – see
'The rites of spring and other pagan ceremonies'), and there
was a general belief that if a barren woman were to spend the
night sleeping on the body of the giant, she would then be
able to have children.

   T. C. Lethbridge thought that the giant we now see
(whom he interpreted as Hercules/Helith/Gog) is the
remaining part of a larger group of figures. He saw, directly and
in aerial photographs, a cloak hanging over the giant's
outstretched arm, and another figure to his right.

Westbury white horse, on Bratton Down, near Westbury, Wiltshire
ST 898516 (167)

Here on the edge of Salisbury Plain where it flows down into the Vale of
Pewsey is the Westbury white horse. Although the horse we can see today
was probably cut in 1778, the site displayed a white horse long before the
eighteenth century. The original horse was beaked (this feature suggests that
it is contemporary with the Uffington horse), and didn't look much like a
horse; it may have been a dragon. Some people have seen the original horse
on aerial photographs, standing immediately behind the present horse and
facing the same way.

Aerofilms

Immediately above the horse on the hilltop can be seen the ditch and ramparts of Bratton Castle, which is said to be an Iron Age hillfort. This is just one instance where a chalk-cut figure has an earthwork formed on the hilltop above it. Although some of these earthworks can be designated as Iron Age forts, and may have been used as such, there is the possibility that these enclosures and the chalk figures stem from a time when man looked to the hilltops not as a means of defence, but to be nearer to the life-giving forces and his gods.

Gogmagog giant, on the ramparts of Wandlebury Camp near
Cambridge   TL 493534 (148)

In the 1950s, T. C. Lethbridge went to Wandlebury to look for the
legendary giant said to be outside the Iron Age camp in the Gogmagog Hills.
To his surprise, by detailed probing he discovered three figures (a man
wielding a sword – Wandil?; a woman – Magog/Epona the Gaulish horse
goddess?; and another male figure, identified as the Sun god and Gog),
together with a beaked horse and a chariot.

His interpretation of the scene was that the demon of darkness had been
defeated by the Sun while trying to stop the progress of the Moon. However,
he also thought that originally there was only Magog (she was 120 feet high)
with the horse and chariot, cut around 200 B.C., and that the other two
figures were added later, around 50 B.C. The fascinating details of Mr
Lethbridge's search, and a fuller interpretation of what he found, can be
read in his book *Gogmagog : The Buried Gods*.

The photograph shows the head of the partly excavated goddess Magog.
The site is now overgrown again.

The Long Man of Wilmington, on Windover Hill, near Wilmington, Sussex   TQ 544035 (183)

This figure bears no resemblance to the giant of Cerne Abbas. He stands tall and thin, his two outstretched arms holding what appear to be two long staffs. He is 231 feet tall, and is thought to be the largest representation of a human figure in the world. There is no real evidence of his identity, and T. C. Lethbridge, who supported the theory that many of the hill figures were connected with Sun worship, suggested that if the Long Man is also associated with the Sun, he could either be opening the doors of heaven after triumphing over the demon of darkness, or holding up two Sun discs on poles, as has been seen on some Scandinavian rock carvings. He has also been described as a Roman soldier, St Paul, King Harold, and other historical characters.

Uffington white horse, near Uffington, Berkshire   SU 302866 (158)

This large chalk figure, 360 feet long from nose to tail, is generally known as the white horse of Uffington, but his strange appearance has caused some people to question whether he is in fact a horse. At the bottom left of the picture is one of those curious flat-topped mounds that are to be found in varying sizes all over Britain. On the righthand edge of the picture is a corner of the earthbank enclosure known as Uffington Castle. Sometimes called an Iron Age hillfort, although it would provide very little means of defence, it is a shallow ditch, approximately rectangular, with earth banks each side, and covers about 8 acres.

Traditionally, every seven years at Whitsuntide the chalk outline of the figure was cleared of grass and weeds by the local villagers, and this scouring was accompanied by the 'pastime' when games and a fair were held inside the enclosure. This ancient practice was discontinued about 1857, and nowadays the site is kept in good repair by the Department of the Environment.

Below the horse in the bottom centre of the picture is a combe in the hills, known as the Manger, and down this slope round cheeses were rolled. All these activities point to the continuance of a pagan festival similar to others described in this book (see 'The rites of spring and other pagan ceremonies'). But what power were these prehistoric people acknowledging in their rites? Was it the dragon power that flowed through the leys? The fact that the strange shaped horse could also be a dragon has been noted by others, and the legend that clings to the artificial mound at the bottom left of the picture, that is called Dragon Hill, is that St George slew the dragon on its summit, and where its blood was spilled, no grass will grow. There is to this day a bare patch on its top.

Also remarkable is the angle of the slope on which the figure of the white horse is cut. It is difficult to see from the ground, but from the air, as in the picture, it stands out clearly. Could it be, as some have suggested, that it was intended to be seen from above, a signal from Neolithic man to his gods in their airborne craft who would then land on Dragon Hill?

The
Puzzle of the
Maze

*'The nine men's morris is filled up with mud
And the quaint mazes in the wanton green
For lack of tread are indistinguishable.'*

A Midsummer Night's Dream

It would seem that at one time Britain had numerous mazes spread over the country, but today very few remain. It does not take long for a maze cut in the turf to become overgrown, and to disappear from sight and memory. The antiquity of those few turf mazes that remain is a matter of much speculation. The mazes formed in gardens by clipped hedges are a recent development and do not concern us here.

Mazes or labyrinths were constructed in the ancient Mediterranean world, and the most famous is the Cretan labyrinth which has not yet been rediscovered, within the intricacies of which lurked the dreadful Minotaur of legendary fame. Other ancient mazes have been found in Finland, Sweden, Lappland and Iceland. These are made from pebbles usually on the seashore or on islands, and some are formed from large stones. In one example, on the southern coast of the peninsula of Lappland, each stone would require several men to carry it. Many of these mazes have been dated to the Bronze Age. On the Scilly Isle of St Agnes, there is upon the westernmost promontory, Camperdizil Point, a maze constructed of small stones, the date of which is unknown, though its name of Troy Town suggests that it is of no little antiquity. 'Camperdizil' may have a connection with 'deasil' meaning 'Sunwise motion', and perhaps indicates the direction of the dance performed within the maze.

In Europe, the ecclesiastical architecture of the mediaeval churches often incorporated a maze in a tile-paved area, so the metaphysical significance was still known at this time, even though to only a few. The most famous that still exists is in Chartres Cathedral in France, and measures 40 feet across. Strangely, though, the mediaeval cathedral builders in Britain did not incorporate mazes into their designs, whereas the turf maze appears to have been exclusive to this country.

Mazes are frequently called Troy Town or The Walls of Troy, and Troy Towns or Draytons appear in many parts of the country. Popular tradition gives the derivation as being that the walls of Troy were so constructed that an enemy, once inside, could neither find his way into the city nor outside again. Some mazes were called Julian's Bower, and this is thought to derive from Julius, the son of Aeneas of Troy, and *burgh* meaning castle or city, the combination giving 'City of Julius', in other words, 'Troy Town'. Other names that are attached to mazes are Mizmaze and Shepherd's Race, and in Wales where the shepherds would cut them into the turf on the hillsides, they were called Caerdroia, the City of Troy.

Although in later times the maze seems to have degenerated into a child's game (the children's street game of hopscotch, often played on a chalked-out spiral shape, is thought to derive from maze games) or provided some fun on highdays and holidays, originally it must have been of profound significance in the initiatory ceremonies of the Neolithic culture and may have been instrumental in raising the subtle life-giving energies inherent in the body of the earth by means of a formal dance paced out along the intricacies of the winding path.

One researcher has suggested that mazes were originally astronomical observatories, deriving the word *troiau* in Caer Troiau or Caerdroia from *troi* meaning 'to turn' or *tro* meaning 'a flux of time'. Patterns on numerous whorls dug up at Troy suggest stars and planets, also a sense of rolling or movement. Harold Bayley, discussing mazes, suggests that 'it would seem highly probable that the knot, maze, Troy Town, or trou town, primarily was emblematic of the Maze or Womb of Life, conceived either physically or etherially in accord with the spirit of the time and people.' Spirals carved on the stones at Newgrange may also represent the Maze of Life, echoing the idea that burial inside elaborate burial mounds symbolized a return to the womb. (For more information on Newgrange, see 'Archaic crosses and carvings'. Burial mounds are discussed and illustrated in 'Earthworks on the hilltops'.)

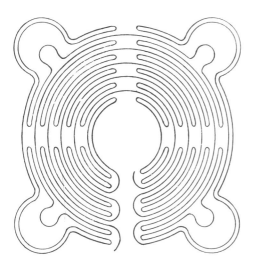

turf labyrinth, Saffron Walden, Essex   TL 540385
(approx.) (148)

One of the largest still to be seen in Britain, this labyrinth is
90 feet across the circle and 140 feet diagonally across the
'bastions' or corner turrets. These and the centre plot are
slightly raised above the rest. This maze is on the east side of
Saffron Walden common, and a few hundred yards away is
another maze, the hedge maze at Bridge End Gardens.
However, this is not of any great antiquity.

Colin Bord

maze at Wing, Rutland SK 895028 (122)

This turf maze in the village of Wing has been well cared for
and is in a good state of preservation. Nearby is a large
tumulus. Ancient earthworks and turf mazes are found
together too frequently for coincidence – another pointer to
their prehistoric origins.

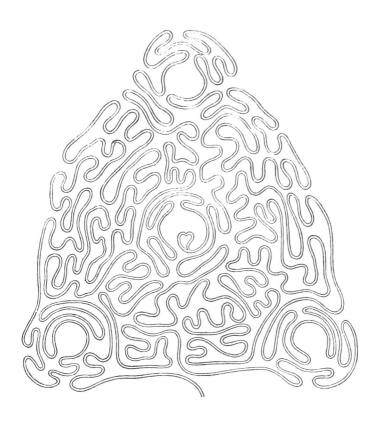

'Troy Town', Pimperne, Dorset

This unique maze was seen by the antiquary John Aubrey,
who wrote in 1686 that it was 'much used by the young
people on Holydaies and by ye School-boies'. On each side
of the path was a 1 foot high ridge. The whole area was
ploughed up in 1730.

'Shepherd's Race', Boughton Green,
Northamptonshire

Until the early years of this century, this maze could be seen
near the ruined church of St John the Baptist, half a mile
from Boughton village. An unusual feature was that the
centre was a regular spiral, the whole being 37 feet across.
'Treading the maze' was a part of a three days June fair which
was granted a royal charter in 1353. The army in a training
exercise during the 1914–18 war decided it was necessary
to dig trenches across the maze, and this practically
obliterated it, time and nature doing the rest.

'Julian's Bower', Alkborough, Lincolnshire
SE 881217 (104)

On the side of a hill is a basin-shaped depression in which the
maze is cut. It is 40 feet in diameter and cut 6 inches deep in
the turf. On the hilltop is an earthwork thought by some to
be Roman, but it is likely to be older. In the early nineteenth
century, the villagers played May Eve games in the maze,
and one villager who was a youth at the time wrote that he
had '. . . an indefinite persuasion of something unseen and
unknown co-operating with them' as they ran along the
paths to the centre and back to the outside.

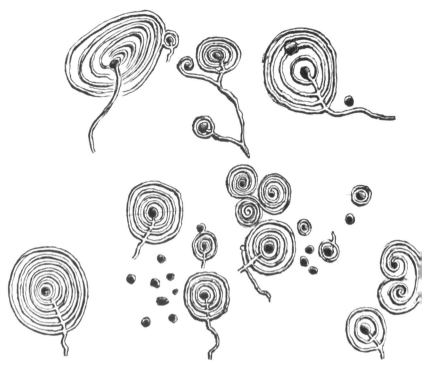

Such carvings as this, called cup and ring marks, are found
on many rock surfaces, particularly in western areas of
Britain. Their purpose is unknown, but their similarity to maze
designs has been noted, and some think there may be a
definite connection between the two. Small labyrinth
designs are found in some continental churches, on the
walls. These can be traced out with the finger, and the cup
and ring carvings may have had the same purpose. (For
more information on cup and ring marks, see 'Archaic
crosses and carvings'.)

These ancient coins found at Knossos in Crete are
impressed with maze designs, another link between Britain
and the Mediterranean.

stone at the meeting of the tracks, near Llanfairfechan,
Caernarvonshire   SH 693722 (107)

This pattern is found scratched on stones in the hills of Wales and the Isle of
Man, and was used by the shepherds to play a game called Trios. It has been
known in Greece for thousands of years, where it is called Triothi. The
connection with shepherds brings to mind the 'Shepherd's Race' of the
mazes. Could Trios be a corruption of the Welsh name of Troy, Droia, or
the Greek name, Troie?

  Although not a maze game, Trios is similar in appearance to the square
mazes that appear on old coins from Crete. It is played by two people, each
with nine counters which they try to place in rows of three. It is also similar
to a game called Nine Men's Morris.

  There is on the Isle of Man a rock carved with a rectangular pattern of
cup-marks which is said to be reminiscent of an ancient game called
Nine Holes.

Trackways and Leys:
The Unseen Power

'*The revelation took place when Watkins was
65 years old. Riding across the hills near
Bredwardine in his native county, he pulled
up his horse to look out over the landscape
below. At that moment he became aware of a
network of lines, standing out like glowing
wires all over the surface of the country,
intersecting at the sites of churches, old stones
and other spots of traditional sanctity.*'

John Michell, in his 'Note on Alfred
Watkins' in the new edition of *The Old
Straight Track* by Alfred Watkins

This revelation took place in the early 1920s, and heralded the rediscovery of the prehistoric 'ley' system. In the subsequent fifty years
or so, much work has been done by enthusiasts to corroborate and
enlarge on Watkins' findings, with the result that new light has been
shed on the nature of the countryside around us.

The basis of the ley system is quite simple – that sites of ancient
importance align. To test the theory, use any Ordnance Survey map
(except of a 'built-up' or mountainous area), scale 1 inch to 1 mile, and
a perspex straight-edge. Choose an area of the map and circle the
following types of site: stone circles, standing stones, barrows, tumuli,
'castles', mottes and baileys, moats, hillforts, earthworks, churches,
abbeys and other religious buildings; in fact anything which is very old
or traditionally sacred – and then try and align some of them along the
straight-edge. You will soon find many three-, four- and even five-
point alignments, perhaps also six-, seven- and eight-point ones. In
order to rule out coincidence, 'ley hunters' stipulate that an alignment
which merits further investigation must have at least five valid points
aligning within a fairly short distance, that is ten rather than fifty miles.

But there is a great deal more to the investigation of the ley system
than alignments on maps of ancient sites. The next stage is fieldwork,
actually visiting the area which is crossed by the chosen alignment and
trying to trace it along the ground. This part of ley hunting is far more
difficult than drawing lines on a map, and a realization of how much the

encroachments of the twentieth century are changing our beautiful land grows very strong when one is standing on a high point and trying to sight along a ley. The winter is by far the best time to do this (except on a foggy or misty day, of course), because there are no leaves on the trees to obstruct the view. Alfred Watkins was luckier than we of the 1970s, for Herefordshire in the 1920s was relatively unspoilt, and he took many fine photographs illustrating the leys he had discovered. However, leys are still to be found in abundance, especially if a rural area is investigated, and a walk along the route of the suspected ley might bring unexpected and exciting confirmation of its presence, such as a markstone now hidden in a hedgerow but standing untouched where it has stood for literally thousands of years; an obvious piece of old trackway; a notch cut out of a distant hillside straight in front of you. All these and many other features of leys are illustrated later in this section.

Although the existence of leys has been proved many times over, their real purpose is still uncertain. Alfred Watkins believed that they were early man's trackways, and his enthralling book *The Old Straight Track* gives the reasons why he thought this. Later researchers believe that this is only part of the answer, and that the leys may in fact follow invisible lines of power criss-crossing the countryside. Early man was aware of this power, which he harnessed for his own spiritual and physical benefit by erecting his 'temples' at certain significant points along the power-lines. Some people who seem to have a particular kind of sensitivity receive shocks, sometimes violent, when they touch certain ancient stones, but the stones don't seem to be 'charged' with power all the time. (For examples of this feature, see Harold's Stones, Trelleck, illustrated in 'The standing stones and circles of prehistory', and also the introduction to that section). It is thought by some people that leys are used, possibly as a power source or navigational aid, by flying saucers or UFOs as they move around our skies. This idea is expanded in 'The enigmatic UFO'.

Although the ley system seems to have been completely forgotten until its rediscovery by Alfred Watkins, there is one possible way in which its memory might have been perpetuated to this day without our realizing it. Throughout the country there are legends and rumours of secret passages linking old houses with monasteries, churches, and other ancient sites, and sometimes the distances between the buildings concerned are far too long for a tunnel to be feasible. May these rumours not be a folk memory of ley lines?

The ley system is very, very old indeed, and it is practically impossible even to hazard a guess as to when the lines were laid out. Many of the markers we can see today are recent when compared with the age of the leys on which they lie, for example churches, but, as has been emphasized in 'The sanctity of ancient sites', these and other sacred buildings were constructed centuries ago on sites then venerated as being of special importance. Thus were the leys perpetuated.

There are leys all over Britain, and there seems to be some evidence that they also occur in other parts of the world. Some are short and local, others stretch for hundreds of miles across the country. An interesting one in England, taking in as it does many sites which are mentioned and illustrated in this book, begins in Cornwall and ends in East Anglia. Starting from St Michael's Mount (see 'The sanctity of ancient sites'), it passes through the Cheesewring (see 'The standing stones and circles of prehistory'), St Michael's church, Brentor (see 'The sanctity of ancient sites'), Burrowbridge Mump (see 'Glastonbury's Temple of the Stars and other zodiacs'), Glastonbury (see 'Glastonbury's Temple of the Stars and other zodiacs' and 'Earthworks on the hilltops'), Avebury (see 'The standing stones and circles of prehistory'), and so on eastwards, following roughly the course of the Icknield Way, through Bury St Edmunds and crossing the coast just north of Lowestoft. These are just the major sites on its route and of course there are many other markers, old churches, earthworks, stones, etc., to confirm it all along the way. An example of a varied Scottish ley is: Birse church (NO 554972) – Aboyne stone circle – St Machar's Cross – Cairn – Upper Ruthven fort – Newkirk church (NJ 435043). These five sites are all within a distance of eight miles, and are in the Dee area of Aberdeenshire. A typical Welsh ley can be found in Denbighshire, from Valle Crucis Abbey (SJ 207442) – peak on Ruabon Mountain – Cross Street crossroads – camp north of Ruabon – crossroads at Eyton – Plassey moat – 1½ miles of straight road – Tushingham-cum-Grindley church (SJ 522464).

As the interest in 'live archaeology' grows, many more people are investigating such intriguing subjects as leys for themselves. There is a regular exchange of ideas in the monthly magazine *The Ley Hunter* (see reading list), and the beauty and mystery of the countryside are being revealed once more to those who will follow the old trackways.

Janet Bord

earthwork near Clophill, Bedfordshire   TL 097374 (147)

This earthwork, marked on the map as 'Castle Hill', is a
typical example of the banks and ditches surrounding a
central mound through which leys often pass. In cases
where the earthwork covers a large area, and consists of
banks and ditches surrounding a huge flat expanse, any leys
passing through the site usually only touch one of the
encircling banks rather than passing right through the centre
of the site. This is because later earthworks often
incorporated earlier mounds or tumuli in their banks, and it
is through these early constructions that the leys pass.

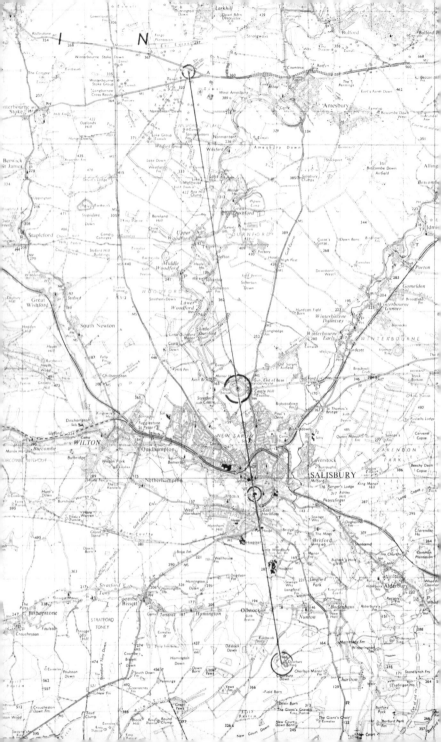

ley through Salisbury Cathedral, Wiltshire

The photographer was standing at the edge of the mound in
the centre of the earthwork called Old Sarum (SU 138327)
(see 'The sanctity of ancient sites' for more information on
Old Sarum and Salisbury Cathedral) when he took this
picture. The graceful spire of Salisbury Cathedral (SU
143295) reaches up to the sky, and immediately behind it
can be seen the earthwork Clearbury Ring on the horizon
(SU 152244). The ley just touches the edge of this earthwork
(as can be seen in the accompanying map); leys customarily
touch the edges of earthworks and do not pass through their
centres. Behind the photographer, the ley continues north
and passes straight through Stonehenge six miles away (SU
122422).

PLATE IX.   MARK-STONES.
    1. Red Lion, Madley.   2. Credenhill.
    3. Wye Street, Hereford.   4. Bartonsham (see Plate VIII).

'*No one can investigate leys in the field for long without being convinced that the way was planted at intervals with stones, which by their size, shape, or appearance, different from stray local ones, made assurance to the wayfarer that he was on the track. . . . The usual characteristic of a prehistoric mark stone is that it is unworked, although of selected shape. Naturally they are placed on, or alongside, the track. The smallest are only a foot or so high, either pudding shape or flat-topped.*'

Alfred Watkins in *The Old Straight Track*

This page from Alfred Watkins' book *Early British Trackways* shows four examples of markstones which he discovered and photographed in Herefordshire and district in the early 1920s. Markstones do not appear on the map, but when a ley hunter is following a suspected ley and comes across a stone such as these, he has received strong confirmation that his ley is genuine. Unfortunately, such apparently useless lumps of rock are no longer left to stand where they have stood for generations, with the result that ley hunters today are less likely to find markstones unless they are searching in truly rural areas which have not yet been assaulted by the march of 'progress'.

THE OLD MAN'S ROAD by W. H. Auden

Across the Great Schism, through our
  whole landscape, Ignoring God's
    Vicar and God's Ape,

Under their noses, unsuspected,
  The Old Man's Road runs as it did

When a light subsoil, a simple ore
  Were still in vogue : true to His
    wherefore,

By stiles, gates, hedge-gaps it goes
  Over ploughland, woodland, cow
    meadows,

Past shrines to a cosmological myth
  No heretic to-day would be caught
    dead with,

Near hill-top rings that were so safe
    then,
  Now stormed easily by small children

(Shepherds use bits in the high
    mountains,
  Hamlets take stretches for Lovers'
    Lanes),

Then through cities threads its odd way,
  Now without gutters, a Thieves'
    Alley

Now with green lamp-posts and white
    curb,
  The smart Crescent of a high-toned
    suburb,

Giving wide berth to an old Cathedral,
  Running smack through a new Town
    Hall,

Unlookable for, by logic, by guess :
  Yet some strike it, and are struck
    fearless.

No life can know it, but no life
  That sticks to this course can be made
    captive,

And who wander with it are not stopped
    at
  Borders by guards of some Theocrat,

Crossing the pass so almost where
  His searchlight squints but no closer

(And no further where it might by
    chance):
  So in summer sometimes, without
    hindrance,

Apotropaically scowling, a tinker
  Shuffles past, in the waning year

Potters a coleopterist, poking
  Through yellow leaves, and a youth
    in spring

Trost by after a new excitement,
  His true self, hot on the scent.

The Old Man leaves his Road to those
  Who love it no less since it lost
    purpose,

Who never ask what History is up to,
  So cannot act as if they knew :

Assuming a freedom its Powers deny.
  Denying its Powers, they pass freely.

Reprinted by permission of
Faber and Faber Ltd
from W. H. Auden's
Collected Shorter Poems 1927–1957

All Saints church, Shillington, Bedfordshire   TL 123340 (147)

As well as being built close by ancient earthworks in many cases, churches
were often built on high ground. The church at Shillington is a good example,
for it dominates a steep rise at one end of the village, and can be seen for
miles around. Such churches make excellent ley sighting points; originally,
of course, the hill itself, which was probably an ancient sacred site, was the
sighting point, for the earliest parts of this church only date from the
thirteenth century, long after the leys were determined. This photograph was
taken from half a mile distance, with a telephoto lens.

St Mary's church, Great Wymondley, near Hitchin, Hertfordshire TL 215285 (147)

Parts of this church date back to at least the eleventh century, and it stands
on the very edge of what is marked on the map as 'Castle Mound'; the outer
banks and ditches can be seen in the foreground. The location of many old
country churches is similar to this one, close by an ancient earthwork (for
more examples see 'The sanctity of ancient sites'). In this case, a ley runs
straight down the aisle of the church, and just touches the edge of the
earthwork. The Norman churches at Hitchin and Graveley, both close by,
are in direct alignment.
    For many centuries, churches which were built along leys continued to be
used as public thoroughfares. Notable examples were the cathedrals of
Canterbury, Worcester, Durham, Norwich, Salisbury, and St Paul's,
London, where it was common practice for people, including those taking
their wares to market, and with cattle and horses, to walk through the
cloisters and the body of the church, even during services. In his long
out-of-print book *Early British Trackways*, Alfred Watkins observes how
often churches were built across old trackways, and a new road was made on
both sides of the church. He gives as examples St Clement Danes, St
Mary-le-Strand and St Martin-in-the-Fields in London, which were built
along a ley. The road now passes by on either side.

Besides being itself a landmark, Shillington church is an
excellent vantage point for viewing 'the lay of the land'.
This telephoto picture shows the tower of Upper
Gravenhurst church, $1\frac{1}{2}$ miles distant across the valley.
Midway between the two points, at the bottom of the valley
and therefore not visible in this picture, is an earthwork
called Church Panel (TL 118350), which may once have
been an island in the midst of swamps.

'*There are times when the power-tides of the Unseen flow
strongly down upon our earth, and there are also places upon her
surface where the channels are open and they come through in
their fullness of power. This was known to them of old time,
who had much wisdom that we have forgotten, and they availed
themselves of both times and places when they sought to awaken
the higher consciousness.*'

Dion Fortune in *Avalon of the Heart*

Alfred Watkins

hollow road, Longtown,
Herefordshire   SO 323289
(approx.) (142)

Sometimes stretches of old
trackway can be found following the
route of a ley, tending to confirm
Alfred Watkins' belief that leys were
used as trackways. This hollow road
leads down to a causeway across the
River Monnow, and ahead can be
seen a sighting notch on the skyline.

Alfred Watkins

skyline sighting notch,
Coldman's Hill, near Holme Lacy,
Herefordshire   SO 556357
(approx.) (142)

'*A straight, hollow track led down the
bank to the river, and was afterwards
found to continue on the map as a ley.
Going down to the river bank at the
point where this track anciently crossed
as a ford, and looking up the hollow
track, I found the section of the track
to show against the skyline as a notch.
What an excellent guide on a dusky
night this notch made when a traveller
crossing the ford wanted the exact
direction to take up the bank, but
could see little but a skyline!*'

Alfred Watkins in *The Old Sraight
Track*

PLATE X.   TRANSITION OF MARK-STONE TO CROSS.

1. Pedlars Cross, Llanigon.   2. Wergins Stone.
3. Churchyard Cross, Vowchurch   4. Churchyard Cross, Capel-y-Fin.
   (Inset, Hole in Shaft, Bitterley).

'*Almost all the wayside and churchyard crosses evolved from mark stones. . . . At Vowchurch, Herefordshire, the churchyard cross (which aligns with the ford over the little river) is clearly an unhewn mark stone ; and above Llanigon, a longstone has been roughly shaped to give it some resemblance to a cross.*'

Alfred Watkins in *The Old Straight Track*

The plate comes from Watkins' earlier book on the subject of leys, *Early British Trackways*. The 'preaching cross' at Bosherston in Pembrokeshire, illustrated in 'Archaic crosses and carvings', may also be an example of a churchyard cross evolved from a markstone.

cross at Bitterley, Shropshire   SO 571773 (129)

*'Bitterley Churchyard Cross has a circular hole through its
shaft at a convenient height for sighting. [See Plate illustrating
"Transition of Mark-Stone to Cross" for a close-up photograph
of the hole]. Mr J. C. Mackay kindly had the exact direction
of this taken for me by sighting compass. It is 28½° E. of Magnetic
N., and this on the map exactly strikes Abdon Burf (or Barf),
the high point (1,790 ft.) of the Brown Clee. Southwards the line
runs through Stoke Prior and Hope-under-Dinmore Churches,
is confirmed in other ways, and goes over the Wye at Belmont
House.*

   *'Bitterley Cross is of 14th century date; it must be the
successor of a sighting stone which in some way pointed the
direction of the ley, and it suggests that sighting along a ley had
not quite died out by the 14th century.'*

Alfred Watkins in *Early British Trackways*

a one-tree hill, Llanvihangel-nant-Melan, Radnorshire
SO 180582 (approx.) (128)

*'There is every reason to surmise that trees were planted in
prehistoric times as sighting marks, although it is obvious that
none so planted can now exist.'*

Alfred Watkins in *The Old Straight Track*

This photograph from *Early British Trackways* illustrates
the use of a tree or clump of trees as a sighting point. The
mound on which the tree stands is quite prominent, but the
countryside around is quite hilly, and the addition of a
single tree causes an important mound to be more easily
picked out.

196

moat near Apsley End, Bedfordshire   TL 122334 (147)

There are many moats throughout the country similar to this one,
consisting solely of a circular mound surrounded by a water-filled ditch.
There seems no logical explanation for them, but Alfred Watkins believed
they were a vital part of the ley system, as the following quotation from
The Old Straight Track shows. '. . . the deduction now made is that the ring
of water was a valuable sighting object, as it reflected light from the sky (and
perhaps at times from a beacon on the ley) when seen from a distance and
from higher ground.'

'*It is becoming slowly apparent that all the vestigia left by the Downland
occupants of pre-Roman Britain, earthworks, trackways, hut and stone circles,
barrows and the scars of ancient mining works, are the ruins of one vast
architectural whole, constructed upon a definite and systematic plan. It is not
only that there exists, could we but grasp it, a topographical key to the unification
of the highways. To possess the archives of this organized Transport Union
would not be the end of the matter. The trackways join hands with the more
ancient of the earthworks, the circles with the barrows, the barrows with the
earthworks, the circles with the trackways, and each of them separately and all of
them together with the mines. These are all the leaves, scattered, foxed, torn and
barely decipherable, of a single volume, part of a set wrinkled deep in time,
written in a foreign language, but very history. And when we have put the
leaves together and then the volumes, and read them from first page to last, we
shall know many things at last of which we now passess hardly a glimmer, and
that knowledge is going to burst the safe and studious walls of the archaeological
hermitage and throw its beams upon the world as it is to-day.*'

H. J. Massingham in *Downland Man*

moated house, Gillow, Herefordshire

Alfred Watkins believed that moated mounds were
eventually used as defensive sites, and dwellings built
on them. In due course, the dwellings came first, and moats
were constructed around them as defence or decoration.

ley through Llanthony Abbey, Monmouthshire SO 289279 (142)

'*A short length of hollow, grassy roadway sights up to a sharp notch on the northern ridge. Planting sighting rods for this alignment, and then sighting backwards . . . the ley passes through the chancel of the original priory (for this is the second building), and then falls upon one of the three deep gullies or tracks which steeply climb the central ridge. It is a good four-point example – the notch, the fragment of old road in the valley, the church on the ley, the steep track up the mountain.*'

Alfred Watkins in *The Old Straight Track*

Alfred Watkins

The spire of All Saints church and the tower of Hereford Cathedral align on the corner of Dinedor Camp. This is one of few photographs showing an alignment clearly, and was taken by Alfred Watkins with a telephoto lens at a distance of four miles.

Alfred Watkins

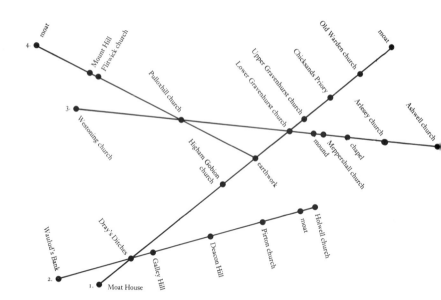

Some typical examples of leys in an area of England not famed for its prehistoric sites.

The four alignments shown in the diagram are all from a small area of Ordnance Survey sheet no. 147, 1 inch to 1 mile, to the north of Luton and the north-west of Hitchin on the Bedfordshire/Hertfordshire border. Many other shorter alignments are also to be found within the same area, but to show too many would create confusion rather than clarity.

1. The longest alignment is 19 miles from a moated house (TL 078240) in the Biscot area of Luton to another moat (TL 160529) at Tempsford. Nine important sites are shown on the 1 inch map, and there are probably others which detailed fieldwork and investigation would uncover.

Following the alignment in a north-north-easterly direction from Luton, it touches the edge of Dray's Ditches (TL 088267), an ancient earthwork of bank and ditch enclosing a large area of land. The next major site is the church of St Margaret at Higham Gobion (TL 104328) which dates back to the fourteenth century or earlier. In the valley half a mile to the north-north-east is The Camp (TL 105333), a roughly triangular earthwork. The alignment follows the western edge of this.

Lower Gravenhurst church (TL 111353) is dedicated to St Mary the Virgin, and most of it dates back to the fourteenth and fifteenth centuries, probably incorporating masonry from the thirteenth century, which suggests that there was a church on the site in the 1200s and possibly before. Half a mile away is Upper Gravenhurst church (TL 113360), dating back to the twelfth century and dedicated to St Giles.

Chicksands Priory (TL 121393), although much changed, dates back originally to the thirteenth century. Old Warden church (TL 137443), dedicated to St Leonard, is at least twelfth century in parts. The final site so far discovered on this alignment is a moat at Tempsford.

2. Waulud's Bank (TL 062247), near Leagrave on the outskirts of Luton, is the starting point for our second alignment. Thought to have been a Neolithic settlement site, there is a bank and ditch still to be seen, though multi-storey flats now tower above. This alignment then crosses alignment No. 1 at Dray's Ditches, next passing through 614 foot high Galley Hill (TL 092270). There are two small barrows on the summit, dating back to Neolithic times. The name of the hill derives from the fifteenth century when it was the site of a gallows.

Deacon (Beacon?) Hill (TL 126298) is the next high point (566 feet) on the alignment, and down in the valley 1¾ miles away is Pirton church (TL 147316), twelfth century and dedicated to St Mary. This is a particularly interesting site, because in a field right beside the church is a large mound. This is marked on the map as a motte and bailey, but that its origins stretch back before Norman times is evidenced in the name also given to it – Toot Hill. (See the Virgo figure in 'Glastonbury's Temple of the Stars and other zodiacs' for more information on toot hills.)

1¼ miles further on is a moat, followed by St Peter's church, Holwell (TL 165333), ¼ mile away. Although this church only dates from 1877, older materials were used and there is a brass dated 1515 inside the church, so presumably a church stood on this site well before the nineteenth century. This alignment of eight points extends for 8½ miles.

3. 15½ miles, in which eight definite sites and two more possibles are marked on the 1 inch map, is the length of the third alignment. Westoning church (TL 028328), dedicated to St Mary Magdalen, was rebuilt in the fourteenth century, but there are some carved stones of twelfth century date. Pulloxhill church (TL 062338) looks and is recent, the present Victorian-style church of St James being built in the mid nineteenth century. However, the site was first dedicated in 1219.

Three-quarters of a mile past Pulloxhill church, the alignment passes through the name Gagmansbury, which looks as though it might indicate a prehistoric earthwork of some kind. ('Bury' often indicates a burial mound, and 'Gag' or 'Gog' was a name for the pre-Christian Sun god. See 'Gogmagog giant' in 'Hill figures – signals to the gods?') The next site is Lower Gravenhurst church, already described under alignment no. 1 which crosses alignment no. 3 at this point.

The church of Our Lady, Meppershall (TL 134359), early twelfth century, stands close by earthworks called The Hills, through which this alignment also passes. The next point is an old chapel (TL 147362) on the other side of Meppershall. Chapel Farm now stands on the site of the twelfth century St Thomas's Chapel Manor, formerly belonging to Chicksands Priory.

Nearly 3 miles away is Arlesey church, early thirteenth century and dedicated to St Peter, and almost another 5 miles further on is what so far appears to be the final point in this alignment, the fourteenth century church of St Mary at Ashwell. However, between these two churches the alignment crosses the main A1 road at a crossroads (TL 224385), which is often a significant feature of a ley.

4. The shortest alignment described here is 7 miles long, with five definite sites, together with two short stretches of road. At SP 993347 is a moat; 2 miles away is Mount Hill (TL 027343), obviously an ancient and artificial construction, and close by is Flitwick church (TL 029342), through which the alignment also passes. This church is dedicated to Saints Peter and Paul, and has its origins in the late twelfth century. Immediately outside the church is a short stretch of road which follows the alignment, with another stretch of equal length on the far side of the A5120 road.

At Pulloxhill church, alignment no. 4 crosses alignment no. 3, the next, and final site being the earthwork called The Camp, 2¾ miles away near Higham Gobion (alignment no. 1 also passes through this earthwork).

Janet Bord

St Margaret's church, Higham
Gobion, Bedfordshire
TL 104328 (147)
(see alignment no. 1)

St Mary the Virgin, Lower
Gravenhurst, Bedfordshire
TL 111353 (147)

This attractive rural church was
originally a chapel-of-ease to
Newnham Priory, Bedford. The
interior is unrestored and peaceful,
and there are mediaeval tiles on the
floor, an ancient stone altar, and a
Jacobean pulpit. (See alignments
nos. 1 and 3)

Colin Bord

203

Colin Bord

From the graveyard of Lower Gravenhurst church can be seen the tower of Upper Gravenhurst church half a mile away (see alignment no. 1). This photograph illustrates how leys are fast being obliterated as more and more development takes place.

Janet Bord

St Mary Magdalen, Westoning,
Bedfordshire   TL 028328 (147)
(see alignment no. 3)

Janet Bord

the church of Our Lady,
Meppershall, Bedfordshire
TL 134359 (147)
(see alignment no. 3)

Janet Bord

St James church, Pulloxhill, Bedfordshire
TL 062338 (147)   (see alignments nos. 3 and 4)

St Peter and St Paul, Flitwick, Bedfordshire
TL 029342 (147)

From the churchyard can be seen, through the trees, the
earthwork known as Mount Hill. Alignment no. 4 passes
through both the earthwork and the church.

The Enigmatic UFO

'*It was the length of two railway carriages with
big lighted windows on its upper structure ;
there was a deep blue-purple light
coming from underneath it.*'

'*It was round, with bright flashing lights on it.
It seemed to have legs hanging down and they had
lights on them, too.*'

'*Silver-grey in colour,
dome-shaped and about 20 feet in diameter . . .
the object had a flat round disc on top,
appeared to have windows in the side,
legs underneath and aerials sticking out from its side.*'

'*The object looked like five round balls
arranged in the shape of a cross.*'

'*The object, about 20 feet long and 10 feet wide,
hovered only a little way above the ground. . . .
It was glowing red with four white lights
along its underside.*'

Flying Saucer Review

Flying saucers, UFOs (unidentified flying objects), UAOs (unexplained aerial objects), call them what you will, are frequently to be seen in Britain's skies. What they are and where they come from, no one really knows, though many claim they have the answer. Visitors from other planets within our solar system, from other galaxies, from the past or from the future, from beyond the grave, from other dimensions, from beneath our seas, from the centre of the earth and coming out through holes in the Poles, psychic manifestations – these and other ideas are regularly offered to explain the many mysterious objects and lights seen in the sky, and sometimes on or close to the ground. The disbelievers are equally free with their explanations – aeroplane/helicopter lights, the planet Venus, a bright star, a satellite, imagination, hoax, 'floaters' in the eye, and so on. But the fact remains that people continue to see inexplicable 'things', and have done so for centuries past.

Sometimes they even manage to photograph them, but this does not happen often, and when it does, the results are never very good. The witness forgets to focus the lens in his excitement, or his nerves cause camera-shake at the vital moment of pressing the button, the result being a blurred picture. But even if the photographer makes no mistakes, things can still go wrong, for it has sometimes been claimed that UFOs emit some force which can fog or otherwise ruin photographic film. Often the UFO is quite distant when photographed, with the result that a small, indistinct image appears on the film, and a camera fitted with a telephoto lens is really necessary to obtain a useful-sized picture on the negative. Pictures taken with amateur cameras usually show a tiny dot of a UFO in a vast expanse of sky, and when this image is greatly enlarged, the grain (which is the physical structure of the negative) is also enlarged, and breaks up any useful details that might have been present. The sceptics complain that no good photographs of UFOs exist, and ask why not, if so many UFOs are buzzing around our skies, but if anyone comes up with a clear close-up picture, 'Hoax!' is the general cry.

There is not a consistent amount of UFO activity throughout the year. 'Flaps' occur in different areas, lasting for varying lengths of time, during which hundreds of people often report having witnessed unusual phenomena. Sometimes these flaps hit the newspaper headlines, as was the case during the autumn of 1967 when the whole country was inundated with reports of 'flying crosses'; and in 1965 the small town of Warminster in Wiltshire was the centre of attention. Countless UFO sightings took place there, and the activity continued for several years. Warminster is in that part of Wiltshire which still holds so many traces of the presence of ancient man, and the town is also a ley centre, in that as many as fourteen leys cross there. (See 'Trackways and leys – the unseen power' for more information on leys.) In the autumn of 1971 the attention switched to Banbury in Oxfordshire, and so it goes on.

It has been suggested that UFOs follow ley lines, perhaps extracting some form of energy from them, or using them as an aid to navigation. However, this is extremely difficult to prove, mainly because of the vagueness of most UFO reports, and the impossibility, in most cases, of being able to pin down exactly where the UFO was. Only low-level sightings, where the UFO was just a short distance above the ground, are really of use in determining whether that particular UFO was on or following a ley, and as there are so many leys criss-crossing the countryside, a great deal of positive evidence is necessary before one can say that it was by design and not by accident that a UFO was on the line of a ley. In 1954, there was a major UFO flap in France, and researcher Aimé Michel discovered that the objects often followed the same route, or were seen at different points along these routes. He called the alignments he found (of sightings during any one day) orthotenies, and the whole story is told in his book *Flying Saucers and the Straight-Line Mystery*. Some work has been done on orthotenies in Britain, and a certain correlation between alignments of UFO sightings and ley lines has been discovered, despite the problems outlined above.

As intriguing as the question 'Where do UFOs come from?' is the question 'Why are they here?' Once again, the answers are many. Some believe that whoever controls the UFOs is up to no good, planning to invade the world, take us over, etc. While a few of the cases reported (not necessarily from Britain) do appear to show hostile intentions, the majority do not, and any injuries sustained by humans on coming into contact with UFOs and their occupants would appear to be accidental. Others believe that we are merely possessions, and the UFOs the craft of our owners, who many aeons ago planted us here and now come back periodically to inspect their experiment.

Right at the other end of the scale are those who look upon the UFO occupants as our saviours, here to protect us from ourselves and from the deadly results of our messing around with atomic power, over-populating ourselves out of existence, and all the other evils of life in the twentieth century. A variant of this idea is that if we do blow ourselves up, we will also destroy or at least harm other planets both in our solar system and outside it, and the inhabitants of the places likely to be affected are here to protect their own interests. A belief adhering to the currently conventional way of looking at things is that the UFOs are here quite simply on a scientific expedition, exploring this planet as we have explored the Moon. Others think that the explanation is not quite so simple as any of these, but may contain elements from all of them, and some other reasons besides, which we could not comprehend even if we were told them.

So despite all the talking and thinking which has been devoted to this phenomenon over the past twenty-five years (since the Kenneth Arnold sighting in the Cascade Mountains, Washington State, USA, on 24 June 1947 first brought the term 'flying saucers' to the ears of a curious public), and despite all the magazines and books which have been produced, the UFOs remain as elusive as ever, quietly doing whatever they are doing, to our detriment or our good, while we struggle with the pieces of a gigantic jigsaw puzzle, of which all the subjects touched upon in this book are small but vital parts.

'Neither a crash-program staffed with twenty Nobel-prize winners, nor computer correlations of millions of poorly observed parameters, nor mental telepathy with superior space beings, nor the organization of hundreds of people into observation squads, scanning the heavens every night with binoculars and a pure heart, will easily dispose of a problem that has eluded our radar, aircraft, astronomers, and physical theories for so long.'

Jacques Vallee in *Passport to Magonia*

Charles H. Gibbs-Smith

'In appearance the UFO was curved and elongated, solid-looking, and of a light colour. Behind it, and seeming almost attached to – rather than emanating from – it, was a "plume", of flame-like brightness; but this "plume" left no smoke trail, or other wake.'

This description is of a UFO seen at 3.30 p.m. on 26 December 1965 near Cappoquin, County Waterford, Ireland, by Jacqueline Wingfield and Lisbet Mortensen. It was a fine, clear day, and they were driving through the countryside by car when they noticed the UFO flying across in front of them. They stopped, and got out of the car to watch as the object flew steadily across the sky, low down, and making no sound. Miss Mortensen had time to take just one photograph before the object went out of sight. This photograph has been printed rather dark so that the UFO (the small white dot left of centre) and its much larger 'plume' stand out clearly.

Fourteen-year-old Stephen Darbishire took this photograph
at Coniston, Lancashire, on 4 February 1954. The similarity
to the objects photographed by the famous American
contactee George Adamski has often been pointed out.

Fourteen-year-old Alec Birch took this photograph from his
back garden in Mosborough, near Sheffield, Yorkshire, on
4 March 1962. 'I suddenly noticed five objects in the sky –
about 500 feet up. They were not moving and they made no
sound. Although the possibility that they might have been
flying saucers did not cross my mind at the time, I took a
photograph of them.' Two of Alec's friends also saw the
UFOs; the Air Ministry's suggested explanation was 'ice
particles'.

During 1896 and 1897 a mysterious airship or airships was/were seen in
many places in the United States, and arguments now rage as to whether
these sightings were of an early terrestrial airship, or of a UFO, and the
amount of evidence on both sides seems to be about equal. Strange airships
were also seen in Britain, the best-known case being Mr Lethbridge's
sighting on 18 May 1909. This took place on Caerphilly Mountain in Wales,
at 11 p.m. What the witness saw was 'a long tube-shaped affair lying on the
grass with two men busily engaged with something nearby'. The men, who
were wearing fur coats, talked excitedly to each other in an unidentifiable
language when they saw Mr Lethbridge, and soon got back into their airship
and took off. Some authors have 'explained' this case as a sighting of an early

terrestrial airship, but this explanation is not acceptable to all, especially in view of the many strange cases recorded in the literature of ufology.

Two months earlier, on 23 March 1909, P. C. Kettle saw 'an object somewhat oblong and narrow in shape, carrying a powerful light' in the sky above Peterborough. Shown here is a drawing of this object, reproduced in a Peterborough newspaper at the time.

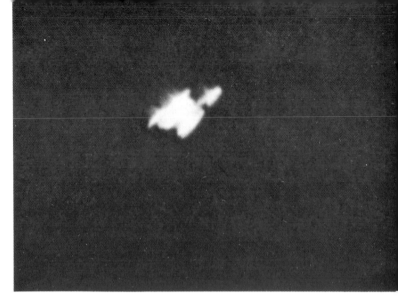

Early on the morning of 24 November 1967, Robert Burke of St Leonards-on-Sea, Sussex, was getting up when 'he saw through his window, high in the sky, a very bright stationary light, of a blue-white hue, which had the habit of becoming intense, then fading to a pin-point.' The light was in sight in a south-south-easterly direction, out to sea, for around an hour, during which time Mr Burke took several photographs.

At twilight on 28 March 1966, Stephen Pratt (aged 15) and his mother were returning home from a fish and chip shop in Conisborough, Yorkshire, when they noticed a single bright orange-coloured light in the sky. They watched it for several minutes, and when they arrived home Stephen fetched his camera and took a photograph. The light seemed to throb as it moved towards the west, occasionally hovering. Stephen's father and brother also saw the light, and his father says he saw two lights. As can be seen, three objects were recorded on the negative.

So Man, who here seems principal alone,
Perhaps acts second to some sphere unknown.
Touches some wheel, or verges to some goal,
'Tis but a part we see, and not a whole.

Alexander Pope in *Essay on Man*

Glastonbury's Temple of the Stars and other Zodiacs

Marked out across the Somerset landscape, within a circle 10 miles across, lies the famed and past fabled Glastonbury Zodiac, ancient Temple of the Stars. This enigma was rediscovered in 1929 by Katherine Maltwood, a sensitive and erudite woman who, by reading the earliest known accounts of the Arthurian Grail Quest, was able to transpose the knights' journeys from Camelot (South Cadbury Castle, 11 miles south-east of Glastonbury) on to the surrounding countryside, beside the Isle of Avalon. By the use of large-scale maps and aerial photographs, Mrs Maltwood was able to delineate figures formed by hills, waterways, old trackways and apparently natural features on the surface of the earth (see accompanying map). When a map of the heavens is placed upon the map of the ground and the major stars in the signs of the zodiac are marked through, they are found to fall within the areas of the figures.

At the top of the wheel beside Glastonbury town and encompassing the Tor lies the ancient air sign of Aquarius. The commonly known sign today is a figure of a man pouring water from a vessel. But the sign used in this zodiac is that of the phoenix, the mythical bird that perishes within its own fire, only to rise again, renewed. This resurrection could have symbolized the new life that the initiate to the pre-Christian mysteries would experience after successfully meeting the trials to be faced in the maze, which is thought to have been upon the face of the Tor. The Tor itself falls within the head of the bird which is twisted round to face Chalice Hill. This hill is within its body, and contains the rust-red water of Chalice Well, said to be the repository of the Holy Grail which was brought from the East by Joseph of Arimathea, to be safeguarded in this already holy site.

The same tradition tells us that it was Joseph who planted his staff upon the neighbouring Wearyall Hill, from which grew the Holy Thorn, a cutting of which now flourishes in the grounds of Glastonbury Abbey, flowering every Christmas and Easter. This was a fitting start to the Age of Pisces, for the hill forms one of the two fish of the Piscean figure, the second fish being formed by a ridge of land to the north of Street. Upon Street itself falls the head of the Aries ram or lamb, who lies with legs folded beneath, looking back over his shoulder towards Dunball on the River Parrett. This river was the means of entry for the traders' ships from the Mediterranean, for the land was undrained in those days, as the lake villages north-west of Glastonbury show, and at high tide the ships could sail up to the Isle of Avalon and beyond, to unload at Ponter's Ball.

Lying outside the circle of the zodiac to the south-west is the Girt Dog of Langport, guardian of the Temple of the Stars. His nose is formed by Burrow Mump, an artificial mound constructed of red clay, the nearest natural deposit being at least three miles away. The ruins of a St Michael's church are upon its summit, as upon Glastonbury Tor, and these two mounds align their lengths upon the same ley which stretches across Britain from St Michael's Mount, Marazion, in the south-west to the east coast near Lowestoft, on its route touching many hills and churches dedicated to St Michael. (For more information on leys, see 'Trackways and leys – the unseen power'.) Upon the dog's head on the map appear Head Drove and Head Rhyne, both drainage dykes, and above its head is Earlake Moor, whilst at the tail end of the figure is the hamlet of Wagg.

Continuing round the zodiac, the folded knee of Aries touches the next sign, Taurus. Only the head of the bull is drawn, by roads, and a ridge of land projecting out from the head towards Combe Hill forms the horns. Of recent years a third 'horn' has been added; the obelisk of the Hood monument has been placed on Windmill Hill, between the horns of the bull. The next sign is Cancer and has, instead of the usual crab, the star ship, Argo Navis. The whole ship is formed by the straight lines of water dykes, a distinct contrast to the other signs which depict living creatures by the use of free-flowing lines. Why there should be a ship here instead of the usual crab seems to be obscure, but Katherine Maltwood links it with the megalithic solar ship, King Solomon's ship in Malory's *Morte D'Arthur*, and with the Padstow hobby horse, the body of which is traditionally an upturned boat (illustrated in 'The rites of spring and other pagan ceremonies').

Within the shape of the ship comes the sign of Gemini, here seen as the Orion giant. He was the Phoenician Sun god, and in Egypt he was Osiris and Horus. The contemporary researcher Mary Caine has seen, by studying the aerial photographs, that within this figure appears another, a youthful, bearded head with a slimmer, angular body. His ribs are plainly formed by the strip lynchets on Lollover Hill, and long hair and beard by the trees and bushes growing around the earthworks of Dundon Hill. Hands are raised above the head in an attitude of supplication. This Christ-like figure within the giant could possibly be of later date. Was it sculpted by intention, or formed by unknown psychic forces moulding the thoughts and actions of the local populace?

The lion Leo is formed by more rivers and roads. The River Cary flows along his ribs, rear leg and foot, ancient trackways that are now roads or footpaths delineate his back, head and front legs, and his jaws are made of terraced lynchets on the side of Worley Hill. His left front paw reaches forward to flatten Somerton, one-time capital of Somerset.

We next move to Virgo who, as we look at the map, appears to be lying on her back, her head pointing towards the west. Her profile and front are outlined by the River Cary, and her hands and her back are formed by roads, and lanes, streams and boundaries. She is the fertile Earth Mother, Ceres, and at her feet we find Wheathill. Within her outline, about two miles south of Babcary, there is the undated earth mound Wimble Toot. It falls within her figure just at the point where her breast would be. Toot or moot hills were points where all from the locality gathered to meet and receive spiritual nourishment. Hence toot equates with teat, as maybe does moot with the Welsh *maeth* which means nourishment. Within her hands Virgo is said to hold a wheatsheaf. This is formed by three lanes and is a rather angular shape for such an object, but it does make a very well shaped cone, and one of the ancient symbols for the Queen of Heaven was a cone. Ancient Cypriot coins show Venus under the symbol of a cone-shaped stone.

Following the virgin comes Libra, commonly symbolized by the scales, but there are no scales on this heavenly wheel. Instead the symbol used is a dove, and this is hidden within the centre of the circle, flying over Barton St David. The emblem of St David is the dove, personifying the balancing power of the Spirit of Holy Wisdom.

Guarding the eastern approach to the Vale of Avalon is the scorpion. His stinging tail is poised above the flank of Arthur's horse (Sagittarius), and Malory in his *Morte D'Arthur* equates this sign with Sir Mordred who, mortally wounded by Arthur, dealt a fatal blow upon Arthur with his sword. As the king lay dying, he was placed upon the barge of death by Sir Bedevere and conveyed to the immortal Isle of Avalon. (See also

'King Arthur and the quest for the Grail'.) The dying king is represented by the sign of Sagittarius, who is here not a centaur but a horseman being pulled over the neck of his mount. This Sun god/king was not only the Arthur of English legend, he was the Assyrian god Assur, the Median Ahura, and the Egyptian Horus. Later he appeared in Christian times as St George and St Michael, both dragon-slayers, and in this zodiacal representation he is being pulled from his horse by a hideous monster with a whale-like body and sinuous serpent's neck. This great fish is outlined along its length by the waters of the Rivers Brue and Old Rhyne. Watchwell House falls on his eye, and Wallyers Bridge is on his snout. His tail lies between the fishes of Pisces, and on some eastern zodiacs a whale is found in place of the fishes of Pisces.

At the head of the wheel is found the earth sign, Capricornicus. His most striking feature is his horn, which is formed by a straight artificial earthwork named Ponter's Ball. In the early days when this country was part of a tidal estuary, this ridge of land, over half a mile long and 20 feet high, would have formed a landing jetty for the traders' ships from the East, who would help fill the horn of plenty and make it truly a cornucopia.

Although so closely associated with the Arthurian legends, this zodiac dates far back beyond the Christian era to that earlier 'Cauldron of Wisdom', that mystic vessel of light and knowledge, which has always been the supreme cause for the sanctity of the Isle of Avalon. In this Aquarian age of resurging sensibilities, this mystic promise now causes a continual stream of youthful seekers of spiritual revelation to converge upon the sleepy little Somerset town of Glastonbury, to the great chagrin of many of its inhabitants.

Of recent years, those researchers who have been concerned with the discovery of leys have also discovered other zodiacs similar to Glastonbury's (these two fields of research are very much linked together – see 'Trackways and leys – the unseen power' for more information on leys). There are four which seem to be fairly well authenticated. They are at Kingston-upon-Thames, Nuthampstead in Hertfordshire, Pumpsaint in Carmarthenshire, and of course the one already described, at Glastonbury. Some others which are suspected to exist but upon which much work remains to be done are at Banbury, Wirral, Durham, Edinburgh, Glasgow and Hornsea.

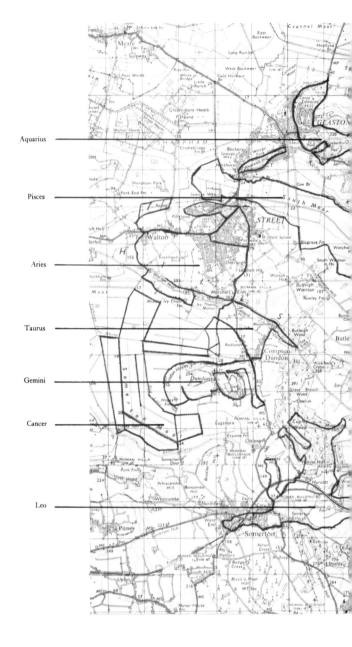

Aquarius

Pisces

Aries

Taurus

Gemini

Cancer

Leo

222

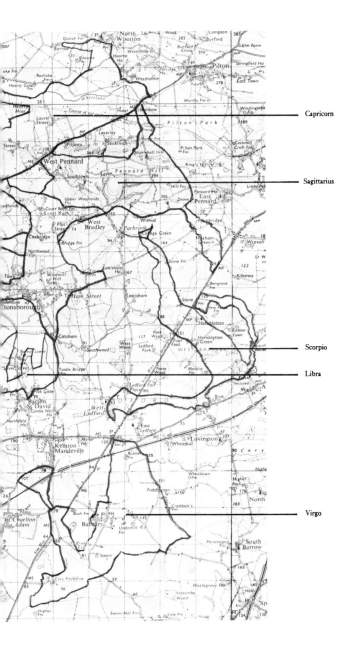

Capricorn

Sagittarius

Scorpio

Libra

Virgo

223

224

This aerial photograph shows the figure of Aquarius as seen from a height of $2\frac{1}{2}$ miles, which is the only way these giant figures can be viewed in their entirety.

It is sometimes thought that if these figures are so very ancient, their outlines would have changed beyond recognition over the centuries. But, surprisingly, the ancient paths and trackways which largely determine the outlines of the figures remain in use to a great extent. Some of them have become enlarged into major roads, while others have nearly fallen into disuse, and have become the green lanes used only by the local country people. Sometimes streams and rivers change course, but this has not happened on a large enough scale to seriously affect the figures. In the same way, names are retained with very little alteration from one generation to the next. The innate conservatism of the British is surely the basic reason for this.

In the lower centre of the picture is the unmistakable outline of the Tor, which is within the neck of the phoenix (see introduction to this section). The 'pilgrim's path' climbs the slopes from the south-west and forms the underside of the neck, which is twisted round from the body in order to look towards the west. On the left of the Tor are the wooded slopes of Chalice Hill, and between the Tor and the Hill are Chalice Well gardens, which are within the wing of the bird. To the left again is a clearly visible square of roads which form the tail and contain the Abbey ruins and grounds.

Thus the three major features of Glastonbury are seen to lie within the outline of the figure that has the greatest significance for these times. As our jaded civilization moves restlessly on, ever seeking fresh sensations and novelties, the figure of Aquarius, which is the phoenix, is an apt symbol for the coming Aquarian Age when mankind must rise again from the ashes of his past stupidities, and all things will be made anew.

Glastonbury, Somerset   ST 501387 (165)

The sacred sites of Glastonbury are seen to be closely placed
in this aerial picture. In the right foreground are the
remains of the abbey church, dedicated to St Peter and St
Paul. The tower in the centre foreground is St John the
Baptist's church. In the middle distance, the hill with the
trees upon its slopes is Chalice Hill; the well is on the far
side, out of sight. Dominating the picture is the Tor,
crowned with the ruined St Michael's tower. In the bottom
right-hand corner can be seen the top of the market cross, in
front of the shops with their sunblinds down. Into the hot
haze stretches the plain upon which Katherine Maltwood
discovered the long-hidden zodiac figures. In the hills in the
far distance lies Cadbury Castle, which is thought to have
been Camelot.

226

Reece Winstone

Chalice Well, Glastonbury ST 507386 (165)

Beneath this cover lies the famed Chalice Well on Chalice
Hill next to the Tor. The shaft was constructed of huge
blocks of stone by the Druids, so legend has it. Twenty-five
thousand gallons of rust-red chalybeate spring water flow
through it every day, and this water is said to have many
virtuous properties. Recently this oak cover was irreparably
damaged by vandals, and has been replaced by one of
translucent perspex, but the significant design in ironwork
has been retained. Some say that within the depths of the
well the Grail lies hidden; its life-renewing properties await
discovery by the Aquarian phoenix.

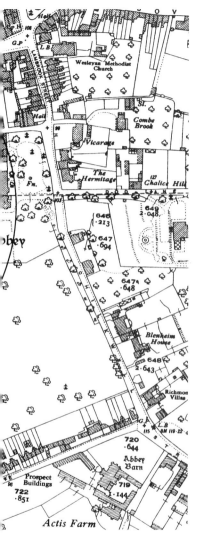

This map of the town and abbey ruins of Glastonbury reveals the findings of researcher John Michell. Using the sacred art of gematria, wherein every letter has a corresponding number, forming a link between literature and mathematics, he has probed into the magical formulae that enabled the geomancers of old to build the abbey to the particular dimensions that would cause the structure to become a temple for the interaction of terrestrial and solar energies, as had been Stonehenge and Avebury before. The centres of the two circles are sites of ancient sanctity, and the circles form the early Christian mystic symbol of the Vesica Piscis. This symbol of the interlocking circles is the basic figure of sacred geometry, and is used on the cover of Chalice Well.

Burrow Mump, Burrow Bridge, Somerset
ST 359305 (165)

Outside the circle of the zodiac, Mrs
Maltwood found a large figure of a dog,
facing to the west. His nose is formed
by Burrow Mump, a large earthen
mound which is partly, if not wholly,
artificial, and is crowned by the ruins
of a church dedicated to St Michael.

King Arthur
and the
Quest for the Grail

*'The ridiculous legends which have been
strung together in relation to this ancient British prince
have made his history little better than a romance.'*

The Saturday Magazine, 31 October 1840

King Arthur is both man and myth, but where one ends and the other begins, it is almost impossible to judge. What does seem fairly certain is that the real Arthur (or Artorius) was a British chieftain who lived around A.D. 500 and gained for himself a place in history by leading British warriors against the Saxons who were landing in their longships from across the North Sea and invading the country, following the departure of the Romans (which took place in the early fifth century).

According to tradition, Arthur was born around A.D. 480 at Tintagel Castle in Cornwall, the son of Uther Pendragon, king of the Britons. His mother was Igerna, wife of the Duke of Cornwall, and Uther gained access to her in Tintagel Castle with the help of the magician Merlin, who used his magic to enable Uther to resemble Igerna's husband exactly. Arthur took his father's place as ruler over the Britons when he was a young man, and was crowned either at Winchester or at Caerleon. Thereafter he fought many battles against the Saxons, assisted by his miraculous sword Excalibur (or Caliburn), which was given to him by the Lady of the Lake. Arthur married Guinevere, daughter of Leodegrance, who gave him as a wedding present a round table which had originally been made for Uther Pendragon by Merlin. This table had seats for all Arthur's knights, and may have symbolized the zodiac, among other things. The knights were often engaged in the quest for the Holy Grail, and it has been suggested that their searches took place in the Glastonbury area, over and around the gigantic zodiac (Round Table) laid out on the countryside there. (See 'Glastonbury's Temple of the Stars and other zodiacs'.)

The Holy Grail for which they searched is itself shrouded in mystery, and there have been many ideas as to what it actually was. In early Celtic legend it was a vessel of plenty, providing whatever food and drink was desired. Later it was Christianized and became the container of the body and blood of Christ. It was associated with Joseph of Arimathea, who had caught the blood of the dying Christ in a vessel, said by some to be the chalice used by Christ at the Last Supper. Joseph later came to Britain, bringing the Grail with him, and it is said to be hidden in Chalice Well by Glastonbury Tor (both illustrated in 'Glastonbury's Temple of the Stars and other zodiacs'). Sometimes the Grail was described as a stone, sometimes the power to ensure longevity and youthfulness in old age was claimed for it. It has also been suggested that the themes of the Grail legends are closely akin to the pagan fertility rites (for examples of the latter, see 'The rites of spring and other pagan ceremonies'); others link it with the search for spiritual perfection.

Arthur's reign came to an end at the Battle of Camlann, where he faced his nephew Mordred who wished to usurp Arthur's power. Arthur killed Mordred, but as the latter died he dealt Arthur a blow which severely wounded him. He was carried in a boat to the Isle of Avalon (thought to be Glastonbury, though it may have been another world whose location no one knows, bearing in mind the legend that Arthur did not die, but sleeps with his knights until he is needed again), and there he died and was buried probably in A.D. 542. Although Glastonbury is the first claimant as the site of Avalon, other possible places are the lost and legendary lands of Lyonesse and Hy-Brasil. Lyonesse is said to lie off the Cornish coast, and to include the Isles of Scilly (see 'The standing stones and circles of prehistory'); and Hy-Brasil is a phantom island marked near the west coast of Ireland on some old charts. This enchanted isle, where the aged could be restored to the full vigour of youth, was sometimes seen as a mirage by people on the west coast of Ireland.

In 1184 most of the abbey at Glastonbury was burnt down, and in the course of rebuilding the monks discovered Arthur's burial place. This site for his grave was the same as that given in an ancient Welsh ballad. At a depth of 7 feet a huge, broad stone was found, where 'on that syde that laid downwards was found a thin plate of lead, about a foot long, in the form of a cross, and on that syde of the plate towards the stone was engraven, in rude and barbarous characters, this inscription: – *Hic jacet sepultus inclytus Rex Arturius in Insula Avalonia.*' (Here lies buried the renowned King Arthur in the Isle of Avalon.) His bones were found in the trunk of a tree 9 feet below the stone, and nearby were more bones supposed to be those of his wife Guinevere.

232

'The king's bones were of large size, so that when his shin-bone was laid to the foot of a very tall man, it reached three fingers above his knee; and in his skull were perceived ten wounds one of which was very large, and looked upon as the cause of his death. The queen's body seemed to be perfect and whole, and her hair was found to be neatly plaited, and of the colour of burnished gold, but her corpse being touched by the finger of one of the spectators, it fell to dust.'

After Arthur's death, his remaining knights were pursued westwards by Mordred and his men (this version of the legend conflicts with that referred to earlier, which stated that Mordred was killed by Arthur). They fled through Cornwall to Lyonesse, but Merlin the Enchanter intervened, there was an earthquake, and Lyonesse was submerged. Mordred's soldiers were drowned, but Arthur's knights were safe on the Scilly Isles, where they spent their remaining days.

The most well-known portrayal of the story of Arthur and his knights is probably Sir Thomas Malory's *Morte D'Arthur*, written in the fifteenth century. Earlier the bards of the French courts had taken the stories of the knights of the Round Table and embellished them, and these versions were told in the poems of Chrétien de Troyes in the late twelfth century. Many of the 'facts' had been extracted from Geoffrey of Monmouth's *Historia Regum Britanniae* (History of the Kings of Britain), written around 1147; Arthur's story was also recorded by the historian William of Malmesbury. The oldest surviving Welsh manuscript *The Black Book of Carmarthen* contains a reference to King Arthur (c. 1150); and the earliest recorded mention of the Round Table occurs in the poem *Roman de Brut* written by Robert Wace around 1155 and based on Geoffrey of Monmouth's history. So many people had a hand in compiling the story of Arthur and his knights as we know it today (of which those mentioned above are but a small number), that fact and fiction are inseparable.

Many places in England, Scotland and Wales lay claim to links with King Arthur, though how many genuinely so, it is difficult to say. The sites of his battles, courts, etc., are much disputed. There are also Arthur's Stones, Quoits, Chairs, Seats, Fountains, and so on. Avalon is generally identified as Glastonbury in Somerset; Camelot as South Cadbury Castle only a few miles away. Camlann may have been by the River Camel in Cornwall, the River Cam in Somerset, or at Camboglanna in Cumberland.

Arthur's ghost haunts the places of his former splendour, and he goes hunting on winter nights along King Arthur's Lane which is a track leading down from the hillfort at South Cadbury. The sounds of shouting and baying hounds are heard. Not far away is a causeway (of which slight traces only can be seen when the conditions are right), between South Barrow and North Barrow, and along this causeway on Midsummer Eve ride Arthur and his band of warriors. They carry lances with glowing tips, and are an awesome sight. The Gower Peninsula in South Wales is claimed by some to be the site of Camelot (Caerleon, named as the site of one of Arthur's courts, is not far away). Here by the sea is a cromlech called Arthur's Stone, and at the full moon a figure in luminous armour, thought to be Arthur, comes from the stone and goes down to the seashore.

The legends of King Arthur, which are far more complex than may appear from the brief outline given here, can be interpreted in many ways; the mystic, esoteric and spiritual all meet here. So much is symbolic, and from these wondrous tales which have so captured the imaginations of people throughout the succeeding 1,400 years can be read much that relates to the past civilizations which have left their mark on our countryside and customs.

King Arthur's Round Table, Caerleon, Monmouthshire
ST 340906 (approx.) (155)

Although thought to have been a Roman amphitheatre, nevertheless this grassy area bears King Arthur's name, for Caerleon is said to have been one of the sites where Arthur held his court. Caerleon is one of the places about which the legend is told that King Arthur and his knights are not dead, but asleep in a cave, ready to awaken when the country needs them. (In Malory's words, *rex quondam rexque futurus* – the Once and Future King.)

This fourteenth century French manuscript, part of 'Le Roman de Lancelot du Lac et de la Mort du Roi Artu', shows King Arthur and his knights seated at the Round Table. In front of them is the Holy Grail, and in this instance it is represented as a ciborium (a vessel containing the consecrated host).

Tintagel Castle, Cornwall   SX 051890 (185)

The legendary birthplace of King Arthur. One version says
that the baby Arthur was washed up by a wave into the arms
of Merlin the magician, who was standing at the foot of the
cliffs. There is a cave on the shoreline below the castle which
is still called Merlin's Cave.

'*But now farewell. I am going a long way*
With these thou seest – if indeed I go –
(For all my mind is clouded with a doubt)
To the island-valley of Avilion;
Where falls not hail, or rain, or any snow,
Nor ever wind blows loudly; but it lies
Deep-meadow'd, happy, fair with orchard-lawns
And bowery hollows crown'd with summer sea,
Where I will heal me of my grievous wound.'

Morte D'Arthur by Tennyson

This painting by Archer of the death of King Arthur typifies the romantic associations which the Arthurian legends hold.

238

Janet Bord

Dozmary Pool, Bodmin Moor, Cornwall   SX 195745 (186)

When Arthur lay dying, he ordered Bedevere to throw his
sword Excalibur into the lake. As this was done, a hand came
out of the water to grasp it – and so it was returned to the
Lady of the Lake. Dozmary Pool is one of several lakes
claimed as the site of this happening.

Britain,
Land of Legends

Britain, the Isle of the Blest of the early chroniclers, has always abounded with legends that reach back into the fog of prehistory. In earlier centuries they were known as basically factual accounts of happenings presented in symbolic imagery, but with the advent of modern rationalism these reports of giants, little people, and monsters were rejected outright as being unworthy of an educated mind. They remained with the ordinary people, however, as part of a great store of folklore, much of which is still available today for us to examine within a broader frame of reference and a greater realization that there are more things in heaven and earth than those who lived during the previous few centuries were prepared to give credit for.

Dragons feature in legends from all parts of the world and are always considered to be completely mythological. But there is a persistence of dragon slayings in the legends of Britain, some of them with so much factual detail that we must seriously consider whether these stories are concerned with relating some very real encounter with a form of animal life which modern zoology has as yet no account of. Such an occurrence is the story of the Loathly Worm of Lambton.

On the banks of the River Wear in Durham are the park and manor house of a well-known family who can trace their line back to the twelfth century, but who are much older even than that. During the fourteenth century the young heir made a strange catch whilst fishing in the river. It was a worm of a repulsive appearance. He flung it into a nearby well and went on with his sport. The creature continued to thrive and presently outgrew the well and returned to the river. The young man went off to the wars and the worm continued to grow apace, frequently leaving the river to forage. It soon began first to annoy and later to terrorize the local population with its mounting appetite. During the day it would lie coiled around a rock in the river, and by night it would come ashore and coil itself around the base of a hill now known locally as Worm Hill. From there it would worry the cattle and devour calves and lambs. The surrounding countryside had become a waste and desolation. Then the young heir returned from the wars. He surveyed the condition of the lands and examined the monster as it lay coiled around the hill. Hearing that others had met the worm in combat and had been defeated, he sought the advice of a sybil, a local wise woman. She told him to fix sharp blades all over his armour, and so prepared he met his adversary on the rock in mid river. The advice of the sybil was well taken, for as the 'loathly worm' attempted to coil around him, the blades caused self-inflicted injuries and so it eventually succumbed, the severed portions being swept away by the river. The sybil had told the young heir that he must kill the first living thing he met on his way home, and he had arranged for a hound to be released for this purpose, but in the excitement, this was overlooked, and his old father rushed forth to congratulate his son. As he could not sacrifice his father, a curse fell on the family, and for nine generations no Lord of Lambton died in his bed.

Clues as to the nature of the 'loathly worm' have recently become available to some individuals who have spent considerable time and effort in investigating reports and films of the Loch Ness monster. They have reached the conclusion that both creatures have many characteristics in common with a new fossil that was found in 1966. This has been named *Tulli monstrum gregarium*, and was found in Upper Coal Age deposits near Chicago. It was a unique wormlike creature with a tiny head and long, flexible neck, and a long, torpedo-shaped body ending in a powerful tail. That it is possible for a species to be found as both a fossil and in living form has been shown by the recent discoveries of live coelacanths from the depths of the Indian Ocean.

Not all the legends that involve dragon-slayings can be said to have a factual basis. The dragon, serpent or worm seems to have symbolized many different ideas at different times in our history. The serpent was originally the guardian of knowledge, and was for a long while associated with those beings who are thought to have descended from the skies to impart the first ideas of civilization to the earliest of men. They also informed him of the true nature of the earth and her need to be refertilized periodically by the correct direction of the earth's natural currents of subtle energies. The channels that these energies flowed along became known in China as Dragon Lines, and the high points through which they passed were the activating centres where the people would gather to direct these energies by ritual and incantation. They became the high and sacred places in every area, where the energies of the earth and those from the cosmos met and were blended into a life-giving unity that could be directed into the surrounding countryside.

During many centuries, the priests gained power and the practices became degraded and ineffectual until the original selfless motives had degenerated into rituals of animal and human sacrifice, the products of fear. A new spiritual impetus was needed, which was fulfilled by the coming of Christianity. When Christianity arrived, the early fathers of the Church quickly realized that their religion could never take the place of the old practices as long as the sacred places of the people were in use, so gradually over the centuries the Christian churches were in-filtrated on to the high places and sacred mounds. The serpent became the evil one, and the new churches on the high places were often dedi-cated to St Michael, symbolic slayer of the dragon, along with St Andrew and St George. (For more information on the coming of Christianity, see 'The sanctity of ancient sites'.)

It is not only dragon legends which abound in Britain. There are those which tell of giants and devils, and especially how many of our ancient stone monuments and earthworks were miraculously con-structed by these powerful gentlemen. More details are given, and specific cases related, in 'The standing stones and circles of prehistory' and 'Earthworks on the hilltops'. The same applies to the legends con-cerning the siting of churches, described in 'The sanctity of ancient sites'.

Certain stretches of the coastline are rich in stories of mermaids and mermen, and although the sceptics will say that the merfolk are really seals, nevertheless some of the legends need more careful consideration than that, especially those which are reliably documented, of which the following is an example. In 1197 a merman appeared on the Suffolk coast near Orford Castle, and this account is from Ralph of Coggeshall.

'Neere to Orforde in Suffolk certain Fishers of the sea tooke in their Nettes a Fish having the shape of a man in all pointes, which Fish was kept by Bartle-mew de Glanville, Custos of the Castle of Orforde in the same Castle by the same space of six monethes, and more for a wonder. He spake not a worde. All manner of meates he gladly did eat, but more greedilie raw fish after he had crushed out all the moisture. Oftentimes he was brought to the church where he showed no tokens of adoration. At length when he was not well looked to, he stale away to the sea and never after appeared.'

Legends can also turn into ghost stories, and vice versa. People re-searching into ghostlore frequently find a particular story which is told locally about a village's most famous ghost, and although everyone knows the story, no one has actually seen the ghost or knows when it was last seen. Thus a single sighting can become a legend, handed down from father to son, with slight amendments in the story as the years pass, but still with a basis of fact. A legend from even further back in time, if repeated often enough and if it involves an animal or human figure, can eventually be told as a current ghost story. Thus is the researcher's job complicated!

Ancient sites often have their ghost stories, and the following quotation from Elliott O'Donnell's *Phantoms of the Night* may be a 'racememory' of the activities which were carried on at stone circles. 'Singing and dancing ghosts are not uncommon in Wales, especially in places where there are Druidical stones. They are generally invisible, and the sounds of their voices, the pattering of their bare feet, and an eeriness in the atmosphere are the only indications of their presence.'

Legends and past customs can be perpetuated other than by word of mouth, in inn signs, for example. A dragon, be it red, green or no specific colour at all, is often seen, alone or being slain, e.g. The George and Dragon. The case of The Black Horse is slightly different, for a recent researcher has found the inns of that name to tell an interesting story. The theory of S. G. Wildman (fully described in his book *The Black Horsemen*) is that there is a connexion between this inn sign and the activities of King Arthur, and that the plotting on the map of the inns called The Black Horse could show the areas where Arthur fought against the invading and encroaching Saxons.

All these examples go to prove that our history is all around us, in verbal form as well as in the physical form of stones and earthworks, and like the latter which need protection from decay, our legends should also be protected. They should be collected and written down so that our descendants will be able to use them for a clearer interpretation of what has gone before.

This imaginative sixteenth century print shows a sea serpent issuing from his cave to attack the sailors of a passing vessel.

243

font in Avebury church, Wiltshire   SU 099700 (157)

On the twelfth century font in Avebury church is this
carving of a winged serpent biting the foot of a bishop. He
in turn is striking the serpent with his staff/crozier. This is
an obvious reference to the battle between the established
'serpent power' worship of the pre-Christian temple at
Avebury, and the new Christianity. Later the serpent
became synonymous with the Devil.

Avebury was one of the more resistant centres to the new
teachings of Christianity; the church, instead of having a
dominant position within the earth circle is outside the
perimeter. (For more on Avebury, see 'The standing stones
and circles of prehistory', where it is fully illustrated.)

SU 188691 (157)

The dragon motif is often used on inn signs. This one is on the borders of dragon country – The Green Dragon in Marlborough, Wiltshire.

Traditionally, serpents coil themselves around the sacred serpent mounds and leave lines scored around the hills. These may in fact be the remnants of symbolic mazes through which the adepts of the serpent knowledge led the initiates up to the sacred place. In this detail from a sixteenth century map are two coiled serpents, possibly indicating the site of such a sacred mound. (See also 'Earthworks on the hilltops' and 'The puzzle of the maze'.)

245

cross shaft in Ramsbury church, Wiltshire
SU 273716 (157)

On this late ninth century cross shaft is a depiction of a
serpent biting its tail, executed in the Viking Ringerike style.
Along his back is a double line of chevron designs. Does this
have the same significance as the pattern on the pillars of
Durham Cathedral (see 'The sanctity of ancient sites') and
the stones at Newgrange (see 'Archaic crosses and carvings')?

Colin Bord

City of London dragon   TQ 312808 (160)

Two of these fearsome beasts flank the road on the
Embankment near the Temple, marking the boundaries of
the City of London. The dragon is traditionally associated
with London, and these carry shields showing the coat of
arms of the city.

The 'monsters' that inhabit the loch (there is thought to be a whole colony of them) are exceedingly sensitive to sounds, and have been known to disappear beneath the surface upon hearing a car door slam or a dog barking on the shore. In 1955, Mr McNab saw a disturbance in the waters, so he quickly fitted a 6 inch lens to his Exakta camera and secured this picture of a monster cruising by Urquhart Castle.

Daily Record

This is the first known photograph of the Loch Ness monster, and started the recent controversy which has continued for nearly forty years, since this picture was taken in November 1933. There was a calm surface on the loch on the sunny Sunday morning when Hugh Gray quickly took this photograph.

248

Associated Newspapers Group Ltd

Probably the 'classic' photograph of the Loch Ness monster. Early one morning in April 1934, R. K. Wilson, a Fellow of the Royal College of Surgeons, stopped his car by the lochside. When he saw this animal moving through the water, he dashed back to his car and obtained this picture with his quarterplate camera, fortunately fitted with a telephoto lens. He estimated the creature's neck to be 6 feet long.

'*It was horrible, an abomination . . . its colour, so far as the body was concerned, could be called a dark elephant grey. It looked like a huge snail with a long neck.*'

This was Mr Spicer's description after he had seen the Loch Ness monster cross the road about 200 yards in front of his car, one day in July 1933 while he and his wife were on holiday by the loch.

Kenneth Scowen

Glencoe, Argyllshire NN 102589 (46)

Scene of a ghastly massacre in 1692, the glen has a
compelling, haunting atmosphere which was probably only
strengthened by the slaughter that took place there. As John
Harries says in his *Ghost Hunter's Road Book*, 'Whatever the
time or season, if, in this valley of angry rock and torrential
streams, the ghost hunter does not feel himself in the
presence of vengeful phantoms he lacks the very rudiments of
the sensitivity for the most persuasive of psychic experiences.'

Crag-y-Dinas, Vale of Neath, Glamorgan   SN 916081 (154)

'In old time of King Artour
All was this land fulfilled of Faerie . . .
I speak of many hundred years ago,
But now can no man see no elves mo.'

Wales, as much as England, Scotland, and Ireland, was and maybe still is the
home of the fairy-folk; the inhabitants of the Isle of Man claimed to be
descended from the fairies. Belief in the existence of fairies was still strong
among the country people of Britain until quite recently, and there are many
stories telling of their subterranean palaces, their hard-working helpfulness,
and their love of music, dancing and mischief.

Sometimes humans were lured into their fairylands, there to be entertained
for what seemed a short while, only to find on returning home that a hundred
years of our time had passed. 'Stories are common of youths who, thus
circumstanced, have returned to find their poor cottages tall mansions, and
their lord's castle an ivy-clad ruin; and who, presently, while conversing with
great grandchildren, crumble into thimblefuls of black ashes.'

In Somerset, the Fairy Fair was generally believed in, one author saying,
'The place near which they most ordinarily showed themselves was on the
side of a hill, named Black Down, between the parishes of Pittminster and

Chestonford, not many miles from Taunton. Those that have had occasion to travel that way have frequently seen them there, appearing like men and women, of a stature generally near the smaller size of men. Their habits used to be of red, blue, or green, according to the old way of country garb, with high-crowned hats.'

Dinas Rock was said to be the last spot in Wales frequented by the fairies. A band of heroes also sleep under the same rock until their valour is needed to change the destinies of Britain. (Any time now?) They were seen by a shepherd boy, who spoke to their chieftain Owen Lawgoch, and later stole some of the treasure hidden in the cave, but when he returned for more, all had vanished, and he found himself alone under the shadows of Crag-y-Dinas. The fairies will by now have been driven out of their home in the rock, and probably the sleeping warriors too, for at the time this picture was drawn, in the mid-nineteenth century, quarrymen were blasting part of the rock.

This figure turned up unexpectedly on a photograph of the altar in Newby church, near Ripon, Yorkshire, taken early in the 1960s by the vicar of the church. He saw nothing at the time he took the photograph, and it was only when the film was developed that the 'ghost' was revealed. The church, only built in 1870, has no ghost story attached to it, and no one knows who or what the figure is, only that it would appear to be about 9 feet tall. The negative has been carefully checked, and no evidence of film fault or fake could be found.

In other cases of UFO and psychic photography, film has been found to be sensitive to 'things' which are not within the range of vision of most humans.

K. F. Lord

Holland House, Kensington, London
TQ 249797 (160)

Built in the seventeenth century, Holland House was
originally called Cope Castle. All but one wing was
destroyed by bombing during the last war, but the influence
of the past has not gone. A recent report tells of a headless
ghost (presumably the first owner's son-in-law who was
beheaded during the Civil War) seen in the grounds near the
house.

   Holland Park in which the house stands also has its
mysteries, and it is said that people have seen their doubles
there. (To see one's double, or *doppelgänger*, warns of the
witness's impending death within a year.)

There aren't many photographs of ghosts in existence, and it is easy to understand why. Ghosts are elusive creatures, and very few people, when faced with one, would react by calmly focusing a camera (if one happened to be handy, which is usually not the case) and taking a picture. On the rare occasions when this does happen, 'double exposure' mutter the sceptics, and so nothing is proved, and the mystery remains. (Compare the ghost photographer's difficulties with those experienced by the UFO photographer, in 'The enigmatic UFO'.)

Well, what do you think of *this* ghost photograph? Is it genuine or not? Taken in 1936 in Raynham Hall, Norfolk, it purports to show the celebrated Brown Lady of Raynham, who was known to haunt the house. Two photographers were taking photographs of the interior of the Hall when they saw a shadowy form gliding down an ancient oak staircase. They quickly took a photograph, by flashlight, and the plate when developed revealed what appeared to be a hooded figure. Experts who examined the plate could find no evidence of fraud.

254

The Rites of Spring
and other Pagan Ceremonies

Visitors and tourists who watch with nostalgia the May-queen and her maidens on the village green dancing round the maypole, or the morrismen pacing out their steps, may sigh for a past when life in England was simpler and merrier. But the ladies of the village, deciding the details for the dresses of the May-queen and her attendants, or perhaps organizing the bonfire committee, might be taken aback to learn that they were participating in fertility rites whose origins stretch far back beyond the beginning of Christianity.

When Christianity first came to these mysterious islands, the early fathers faced the almost insuperable task of weaning the people away from their age-old beliefs and practices. That they succeeded only in part and very slowly is evidenced by the numerous rites and ceremonies that are still practised as traditions, though in a much garbled form, even today. In the same way that they built their churches within the boundaries or close by the pre-Christian sacred sites, so they infiltrated the rituals and ceremonies of the people by declaring that these dates were saints' days and making them known as holydays. In this way they succeeded in eroding the practices and beliefs of the native population, even though this took many hundreds of years to accomplish. Due to the natural wit and resilience of the locals, they were not entirely successful, though the manner and intent with which the rites are practised today have lost all vestiges of their original power.

One ceremony that has survived with a certain spontaneity in some country districts is that of the first day in May. In many villages and towns in England the May Day celebrations take the generally recognized form of a maypole set up on the village green, around which dance the young people, while the May-queen and her attendants sit at the foot. Though picturesque and reminiscent of the popular idea of Merrie England, this form of May Day celebration was largely introduced in the last century in an attempt to revive the mediaeval holiday. In those times nearly every town and village had its own maypole, which was a permanent fixture and a focal point of the May Day celebrations. Today a few villages have such a maypole, which is refurbished from time to time with garlands and flowers and is periodically repainted, often with a spiral design in red and white, colours that appear not infrequently in these remnants of the ancient rites.

Further back in history before the permanent maypole was adopted, the custom was for the young people of the village to go out to the woods on May Eve and, having paired off to spend the night in 'pleasant pastimes', they would then meet again by the light of the dawn to cut down a tree and set it up in the village to be decorated. Another variant was to return with fresh green branches which were used to decorate the houses for the ensuing festivities. These customs symbolized the bringing to each house and to the village of the fertilizing spirit of vegetation. Very often there was a procession that went from house to house carrying green boughs in order to bring the revivified spirit of spring to the crops and cattle, and they would be thanked and rewarded by the householder with a suitable gift of produce. The chief participant in these ceremonies was the May-king or queen, who symbolized the fructifying spirit of the spring vegetation.

Though the celebration of the May Day festival is a dying tradition, that of morris dancing seems to have received fresh impetus of recent years. When or why morris dancing started, nobody knows, but it is as much a part of the English landscape as are the white horses on the Wessex hills. Morris dances are traditionally performed outdoors in the spring or summer, sometimes with May Day festivities, and they were often performed in the churchyard or even in the church itself. The sixteenth century writer Phillip Stubbes tells how morris dancers sometimes entered the church during a service, and how the congregation would 'mount upon the formes and pewes to see these goodly pageants'. At this time it was still customary for the people, after divine service was finished, to sing and dance in church on certain holydays and festivals. The Horn Dance of Abbots Bromley is performed only once a year, and may be even older than the morris dances. It would seem to hark back to the age when man was a hunter, and a dance wearing animal skins and horns was a prelude to a successful chase.

In the Derbyshire villages there is a tradition of dressing and blessing the wells, either during May or at the Midsummer festival. This is a pre-Christian propitiation of the water spirits when the local population would bring greenery and flowers to the well. Today elaborate pictures with a Biblical theme are formed from petals, beans, stones and other natural materials pressed into large trays of damp clay which are then erected over the well. There are about fourteen towns or villages which do this, the best known being Tissington which has five wells decorated.

Another custom of pagan origins is known as church clipping, which means to clasp or embrace. The parishioners clasp hands and walk round the church in a clockwise direction, or they form a circle and advance and retreat three times. This is sometimes thought to be descended from the Roman festival of Lupercalia because that too included a sacred dance round the altar. But dancing was an integral part of the pre-Christian religion in these islands long before the Romans invaded. In Painswick, Gloucestershire, clipping the church is still carried out, followed by an open-air clipping sermon, delivered from the base of the church tower. The ceremony was still practised in Birmingham in 1800, and at many other churches throughout the nineteenth century. But only a few revivals remain today.

The fathers of the Church also adopted the custom from much earlier times of blessing the crops. This occurs in different parts of the country on Rogation Day, which falls before Ascension Day near the beginning of May. This ceremony is usually combined with the more recent one of beating the bounds, when the boundaries of the parish are walked round and certain standing stones or other landmarks are beaten with sticks. It is said that a few centuries ago, small boys were beaten at each mark point in order to impress upon them the boundaries of their parish.

A custom that seems to be unique is that practised at the village of Shebbear in Devon, where, on the evening of 5 November, the men turn over a large stone, which is 6 feet long and 2 feet by 4 feet in girth. Failure to turn the stone would bring disaster on the village, so the legend goes. This stone rests near the churchyard wall, due east of the church and south of a large, ancient oak tree, and is of a composition not found in the locality. The probability is that the church was built on a pre-Christian sacred site, as so many of our churches were, and this stone is either a remnant of a circle, or a standing stone that has now fallen.

Another tradition that has no generally accepted origin is that of the ball game, several versions of which take place annually in different parts of the country. On 6 January in the village of Haxey in Lincolnshire, there is a traditional struggle between two teams for a rolled-up piece of leather termed the Hood. The players wear top hats decorated with flowers, and at one time wore red jerkins, though now they settle for something red in their dress. Before the game starts, one of the participants with a blackened face, known as the Fool, stands on an old stone outside the parish church and recites a story relating how the custom was started in the thirteenth century. While he does this the strips of paper which hang down his back are set alight, and paper and straw are burned at his feet. Then the villagers go to the top of a hill and the game starts. The setting alight of the Fool and other details seem to suggest that the origins of this ceremonial game go back far beyond the thirteenth century, perhaps even to a time when human sacrifice was still practised in this country.

In Scotland, 2 February is a day when ball games are played. At Jedburgh all work stops, schools have a holiday, and a swaying mass of humanity fills the streets, all grappling for a small ball in an attempt to carry it to the other end of the town. In Cornwall the first Monday in February is the feast day of St Ia, the patron saint of St Ives, where the children play a traditional game with a silver ball from 10.30 until mid-day. A similar sport takes place between the villages of St Columb Major and St Columb Minor, also with a silver ball. Even more strenuous is the Hallaton bottle kicking game in Leicestershire, which is a rough free-for-all, the object of each team being to get three small wooden barrels, the 'bottles', into the territory of the respective teams, which consist of men from the villages of Hallaton and Medbourne. Before the start of the game there is also a traditional scramble for pieces of hare pie on the site of Hare Pie Bank.

Ball games of great antiquity and of a religious ritual nature have been found in many parts of the world, and there is a possibility that these traditional scrambles that are still practised today would be found to have a similar ancestry, could we but trace them to their origins. Ball games of obvious pagan ancestry even took place within the church itself, as the following extract from the Revd Geo. S. Tyack's *Lore and Legend of the English Church*, published in 1899, shows.

'One of the most extraordinary customs, as it seems to us, in connection with the choir is the practice, once in vogue, of playing at ball in church at Easter. Among other places it is recorded to have taken place at Chester Cathedral on Easter Monday. The origin of the usage is obscure, though it has been supposed to be not distantly related to the more general Easter custom of presenting coloured eggs to one's friends. However it arose, it was conducted in a fashion which implies that it had some religious significance, and was in fact considered at its commencement as a religious ceremony. The deacon received the ball, and immediately began to chant an antiphon, moving meanwhile in a stately step in time to the music; then with his left hand he tossed, or handed, the ball to another of the clergy; when it had reached the hands of the dean, he threw it in turn to each of the choristers, the antiphon, accompanied by the organ, meanwhile continuing. The statutes of the cathedrals regulated the size of the balls used in this strange rite. In many places there is a tradition still that the game of football is especially appropriate to Easter Monday; and in several towns until quite recent times that game was played in the streets by a promiscuous concourse of people on that day. It is natural to imagine that there may be some common origin to this and to the practice just described.'

Fire always played an important part in the pre-Christian rituals and there are probably more vestiges of our Sun/fire-worshipping ancestors in our present calendar and traditional observances than any other aspect of pagan rites. Midsummer Eve has always been a fulcrum for the Sun worshippers. Until recently, the villagers of Leusdon, Devon, would on this day roll a cartwheel down the slopes of the nearby Mel Tor. If they had continued to cover the wheel with pitch and bind straw around it before setting fire to it and sending it bounding and spinning down the hillside, an obvious symbol of the flaming Sun disc, as their forefathers undoubtedly must have done, then perhaps the custom would not have died out so rapidly. In many parts of Austria and Bohemia this custom was still being enacted in the last years of the nineteenth century, and in some remote areas may even still be done today.

Allied to this custom, there are others in which objects are rolled down the sides of hills. On Whit Monday on Cooper's Hill, Birdlip, Gloucestershire, a large cheese is set in motion, and as it gathers momentum the local boys race after it in an endeavour to catch it and claim the prize. In various parts of the country Easter is still a time for pace egging, when eggs dyed in bright colours are rolled down hillsides. As the egg is a symbol of fertility and is still used in Easter confectionary, the pre-Christian connexion need not be argued.

To return to the midsummer fires, we note that in the early years of this century there was a revival in Cornwall of the custom of lighting a chain of bonfires from one end of the county to the other, with a suitable ceremony spoken in the Cornish language, while in the village of St Cleer there seems to have been a continuous tradition for thousands of years of a huge fire ablaze on Midsummer's Eve, into which flowers and an oak sickle are cast. The earliest recorded name of the parish was St Clair, and this is thought to be derived from Sin Clair meaning the Holy Light, a confirmation of the antiquity of the Midsummer fire.

Before our calendar was changed, 12 January was New Year's Eve, and on this date at Burghead in the north of Scotland, Burning the Clavie is enacted. Here a blazing tar barrel is paraded round the village and each house presented with a piece of burning wood. The barrel is then taken to a high place where it is used to make a large fire; the embers from the fire are in great demand, as they have been for countless centuries from similar ritual fires across Europe. Kept in the house, they were considered to protect it from lightning, and planting pieces in the fields would ensure fertility and a fine crop. In Burghead, those who obtain brands from the fire carry them home to kindle a New Year Fire in their own grate, a practice which has its roots in the pagan Need Fires, which were lit only at such times of distress as an epidemic of the cattle. On these occasions all fires and lights in the neighbourhood were extinguished and the Need Fire was kindled by means of friction of wood, thus it was untainted. The cattle were driven through the smoke, and the people jumped across the flames three times. Then the ashes were taken to be scattered on the fields, and live embers were taken home to rekindle the hearth fire.

Two other dates on which fire festivals were held are the eve of 1 May, which was Beltane, and the Samhain festivities on the eve of 1 November. Of the former there seems to be no trace left, though many other May Day celebrations have survived in various forms. The only remnant that we may have left from the once widespread Samhain fires is that of Guy Fawkes Night on 5 November. In Lewes, Sussex, there is a large celebration organized by Bonfire Societies, which has a strong early seventeenth century anti-Catholic flavour (Guy Fawkes was a Catholic who in 1605 made an unsuccessful attempt to blow up the King, James 1, and Parliament by hiring a cellar under the Houses of Parliament and filling it with barrels of gunpowder). Other towns in Sussex also celebrate the night with great enthusiasm, and indeed the length and breadth of England seen from the air must present a vision of long ago, as dusk falls and the tiny pinpoints of light blaze up first in twos and threes, then dozens, until there are hundreds of gleaming beacons blazing across the land. Although we are thousands of years away from our ancestors, we still respond to the living, dancing flame.

The origin of fairs

A sheep fair was for centuries held on 18 September within the prehistoric camp on Woodbury Hill, Dorset, and it is this same fair which features in Thomas Hardy's novel of Wessex, *Far from the Madding Crowd*.

'This yearly gathering was upon the summit of a hill which retained in good preservation the remains of an ancient earthwork, consisting of a huge rampart and entrenchment of an oval form encircling the top of the hill, though somewhat broken down here and there. To each of the two chief openings on opposite sides a winding road ascended, and the level green space of ten or fifteen acres enclosed by the bank was the site of the fair.'

The origin of fairs is generally considered to have been in pagan times when people met to buy and sell their produce and cattle, and although this did undoubtedly happen, there are some students of these matters who think it very likely that the start of such gatherings occurred in times even earlier. The earliest records we have of fairs show that they were held on hills or mounds, usually within prehistoric earthwork banks, such as are termed castles or hillforts (see 'Earthworks on the hilltops'), or within the confines of a churchyard. Many of these were pre-Christian sacred sites converted by the early Christians to their own use. (See 'The sanctity of ancient sites'.)

Until the last century some country districts observed what must have been the remnants of forgotten pagan rites on days which had been converted to Christian holydays. On Palm Sunday in Wiltshire the villagers of Avebury made their way to the top of that enigmatic earthen mound Silbury Hill, 'to eat fig cakes and drink sugar and water', and in the early years of this century the local populace would, also on Palm Sunday, climb Cley Hill, Wiltshire, to play a ball game within the earthwork on the summit. A few miles south of Avebury is Tan Hill, sometimes known by its Christianized name of St Anne's Hill, where until recently a fair was held every 6 August. Tan was the name of an ancient fire/Sun god, and such syllables as Tin, Tan, Ten and Tein in a name can indicate a former site where their deity was worshipped, as in Tanhill at Midhurst, Sussex, which has a chapel dedicated to St Anne on its summit.

The old sacred sites which had been Christianized by having a church built upon them were still considered by the local people to be the appropriate places for their festivities. The Church officials thought it diplomatic to encourage this practice, as shown by a letter from Pope Gregory in 601 who wrote that on the anniversary of the church's saint's day, 'booths be constructed' in the area of the churchyard, to celebrate the festival 'with religious joyousness'.

The high and holy places of the land were the sites of rituals of a religious nature, ceremonial fires, ball games (which are also found in other parts of the world, notably among the Aztecs of Mexico), and dances designed to raise and channel the life-giving essence of the earth and bring health and fertility to land, cattle and men. As the Christians adopted and converted the old sites, the days of the pagan festivals were changed to saints' days, and all but the most blatant pagan rites were Christianized and included in the Christian ritual. The people continued to meet at their sacred sites, and after the Christian ceremony would stay to transact their business and hold their sports within the sacred area, which was by then the circular churchyard, or in some cases the earthwork near by.

In 1285 the statutes of Winchester forbade the holding of markets and fairs in churchyards, and in 1368 Archbishop Langham forbade not all fairs and markets in churchyards but only those held on Sundays. Bishop Richard Poore at Salisbury in the thirteenth century prohibited 'dances or vile indecorous games which tempt to unseemliness', and as late as 1571 the Archbishop of York had to prohibit Christmas and May games and morris dances in churches and churchyards during 'the time of divine service, or of any sermon'; presumably at other times the clergy had to turn a blind eye to the continuance of the old practices.

May Day at King's Lynn, Norfolk

We've been rambling all the night,
And sometime of this day;
And now returning back again,
We bring a garland gay.

A garland gay we bring you here;
And at your door we stand;
It is a sprout well budded out,
The work of our Lord's hand.

This song was sung by the children of the villages of Essex
(and may even still be sung) on the first day of May as they
carried their garlands of may blossom from door to door, as
seen in this woodcut. Similar customs are observed in other parts
of Britain.

The eve of May Day was the ill-famed Walpurgis Night
when the power of evil was abroad. This was the time to
light the Beltane fires on the high places and to dance
around them crying 'Burn the witches, burn the witches'.
Loud noises were also used to drive these malevolent
creatures away, such as the horns being blown in the picture.

Reece Winstone

maypole dance, Kingsteignton, South Devon   SX 869735 (188)

This scene of a youthful maypole dance photographed a few
years ago is typical of the present-day celebrations. Most of
these festivals are revivals of the last century or later, and the
mood is idyllic and pastoral rather than rumbustious and
earthy. This maypole dance is held on Whit Tuesday, when
there is a Ram Fair at Kingsteignton. A traditional
procession moves through the streets with the decorated
carcase of a lamb, which is later roasted in the open air.
Local tradition says that this was originally a pagan sacrifice.

Jack-in-the-Green

Green George we bring,
Green George we accompany,
May he feed our herds well,
If not, to the water with him.

A central figure in the May Day festivities was Jack-in-the-Green, who was completely covered by a bell-shaped wickerwork frame in which were twined branches, leaves and flowers. He was taken round the village with music and song, and at the end of the ceremonies was symbolically drowned or otherwise killed.

This ritual killing of the May-king, Green Man, Green George or Jack-in-the-Green (all traditional names for the same character) appears to be a strange way in which to treat the bringer of fertility. In many parts of the world, the king, who was considered to be the incarnation of a divine being, was put to death at the end of a fixed term, or when his powers were thought to be waning. The philosophy and intention behind this practice was that the divine spirit must be released from the frail physical body within which it is held, in order to reincarnate in a revitalized form, and in the case of the fertility god to be able to spread his life-giving powers throughout the land.

TL 213286 (147)

This inn sign in the village of Great Wymondley,
Hertfordshire, perpetuates the Green Man, although here he
has become a rather bucolic character, not quite in keeping
with the mysterious spirit of the trees that appeared on May
Day.

Padstow hobby horse, Cornwall   SW 919752 (185)

On May Day the town of Padstow is decorated, and the hobby horse parades
the streets led by the 'teaser' (on right of picture). The hobby horse is a
boat-shaped frame covered with black oilcloth on which is a head, decorated
with the colours traditionally associated with resurgent life, red and white.
As he dances through the crowd, the horse sometimes bumps into the women
and girls, intentionally, and sometimes grabs at them, a reminder of the
fertility symbolism that was an integral part of this old ceremony. Why a boat
should be called a hobby horse is obscure, but it may well be derived from the
same ancient horse god whose image is cut on many of the hillsides in the
south-west of England (see 'Hill figures – signals to the gods ?').

Other hobby horses appear at Minehead, Abbots Bromley (see the Horn
Dance illustrated elsewhere in this section), and Folkestone. He was also seen
in the Yuletide celebrations when either a horse's skull or a wooden horse's
head, decorated with coloured ribbons, was carried from door to door on a
pole held by a man beneath an enveloping sheet, who was known as Old Hob.

267

Reece Winstone

morris dancing, Bampton, Oxfordshire SP 314033 (158)

The only certain thing known about morris dancing is that it is very, very old, how old nobody knows, but there is little doubt that its origins were in the time of our ancestors when dances were performed all over the land to aid the flow of the fertilizing currents in the springtime.

Here are seen the morris dancers of Bampton, who on Whit Monday tour the village, stopping at various points. In this picture they are on the village doctor's lawn. They perform their dance while the 'fool' encourages them with beatings from a bladder tied to a stick. Another character, peculiar to this particular group, carries round a cake on the end of a sword, and a piece of this cake is awarded to anyone putting a donation in the collecting box. On the left of the picture is the old fiddler who provides the music. This is augmented by the sound of the bells which the dancers have strapped to their legs.

Horn Dance at Abbots Bromley, Staffordshire   SK 080245 (120)

Another ceremonial dance which may have its origins in the ages when our
pagan forebears were hunters is this Horn Dance, held annually on the
Monday following 4 September at Abbots Bromley. There are six sets of
horns, the largest weighing over 25 lbs, and they are kept in the parish church
for the rest of the year. Other characters who have joined the troupe in later
centuries are the hobby horse, seen in the centre background of the picture,
the fool with his cap and bells, seen between the dancers on the left of the
picture, Maid Marian, in white, and Robin Hood with bow and arrow. They
are on either side of the hobby horse, partly hidden by the dancers.

The Horn Dance is part of the annual wake (fair), itself an ancient
celebration most likely stemming from the Lugnasad fire festival of 1 August
which was dedicated to the Sungod Lug and converted by the Christians into
Lammas Day.

A famous ghost story from Windsor Park may have associations with the
Horn Dance. Herne the hunter is said to haunt a blasted oak in the forest,
and the ghost is vividly described by W. Harrison Ainsworth in his book
Windsor Castle : 'a wild, spectral object, possessing a slight resemblance to a
human being, clad in the skin of a deer and wearing on its head a sort of
helmet, formed of a skull of a stag, from which branched a large pair of
antlers. It was surrounded by a blue phosphoric light.'

Are both Herne's ghost and the horn dancers survivals of far distant
rituals?

Marshfield mummers, Gloucestershire   ST 780737 (156)

The traditional time for the mummers to act their old dramas is around
Christmas. In past centuries, they would give a performance in all the large
houses of the locality, and also in the village square. These mummers are at
Marshfield, a village in the Cotswold hills, and their costumes are made from
strips of paper. A few centuries ago, every town and village had its group of
mummers who appeared on Christmas and May Days with their simple
rustic performance. Today very few are left, though there have been some
revivals when the words of the plays have been preserved in writing;
traditionally they were passed on verbally from one generation to the next.

The theme is generally the same as in the Green Man or Green George
ceremony of May Day, that is, of death and rebirth of nature. There is in fact
usually one character called St George, or sometimes King George or Prince
George, and another is the Turkish knight who is killed and resurrected by
the doctor. These mummers' plays had their origins in the same pagan times
as the Green Man rituals when human sacrifice was part of the annual round
of life, and in mankind's attempt to regain the favour of the gods who seemed
to have deserted them.

It was reported in 1804 that dancing and games at feasts and revels 'were universal in the churchyards of Radnorshire and very common in other parts of Wales'. In Shropshire, games in the churchyard of Stoke St Milborough were still held in 1820. The old drawing above gives an idea of how such festivities looked. By this time, it was simply tradition, the original purpose having been long forgotten.

carrying the lighted holly tree

A great event of the ancient world was the midwinter fire festival, to celebrate or encourage the rebirth of the waning Sun. Later this was Christianized into the Christmas celebrations. In this old drawing, the villagers of Brough in Westmorland are carrying a burning holly bush in procession. Such burning brands were carried around the fields in many parts of the country in order to ensure fertility during the coming year.

271

bringing in the Yule Log

This was the winter counterpart to the Midsummer fire festival, and due to
the climate was held within the house rather than outdoors. On Christmas
Eve, the 'Yule-log' or 'Christmas-block' was brought into the house with
ceremony and festivity, the custom being to light it with a fragment from the
Yule log of the previous year. In some districts the ashes were scattered over
the fields to ensure their fertility, and the remains kept in the house to protect
it from fire and lightning. Although Father Christmas is a comparatively
recent addition to the Christmas festivities, it is interesting to see that he
wears red and white clothing. These two colours represent the Sun, and
appear frequently in these ancient Sun/fire festivals.

Up-Helly-Aa   HU 476415 (4)

This present-day fire festival takes place in Lerwick in the Shetland Isles at the end of January, and probably derives from the ancient Oimelc celebration of 1 February. The highpoint of events is a torchlight parade with a replica of a Viking longship which is hauled down to the seashore where the blazing torches are ceremoniously thrown into the vessel.

The main celebration of the Scottish midwinter is not 25 December as further south. The eighteenth century post-Reformation Church considered this to be a pagan and Romish celebration, and forbade its observance. This is why the New Year and the subsequent days are the climax of midwinter in Scotland, and the traditional festivals were transferred to these days.

273

Selected Reading List

GEOFFREY ASHE (ed.)   *The Quest for Arthur's Britain* Pall Mall Press 1968, and Paladin paperback

DENNIS BARDENS   *Ghosts and Hauntings* Fontana paperback 1967

HAROLD BAYLEY   *Archaic England* Chapman & Hall 1919. Deciphering prehistory from megaliths, customs, place-names and superstitions.

CHARLES BOWEN (ed.)   *The Humanoids* Neville Spearman 1969. A survey of worldwide reports of landings of unconventional aerial objects and their alleged occupants.

K. M. BRIGGS   *The Fairies in Tradition and Literature* Routledge & Kegan Paul 1967

ROY CHRISTIAN   *The Country Life Book of Old English Customs* Country Life 1966

Discovering   series, published as paperbacks by Shire Publications. Relevant titles include *Discovering Hill Figures, Discovering English Customs and Traditions* and *Discovering Mermaids and Sea Monsters*. The 'Discovering Regional Archaeology' series includes guides to the archaeological sites of the following areas: *North-Eastern England, North-Western England, Central England, Eastern England, The Cotswolds and The Upper Thames, Wessex, South-Western England*.

ESTYN EVANS   *Prehistoric and Early Christian Ireland, A Guide* Batsford 1966

RICHARD FEACHEM   *A Guide to Prehistoric Scotland* Batsford 1963

Flying Saucer Review   edited by Charles Bowen (21 Cecil Court, Charing Cross Road, London WC2), internationally acknowledged to be the best magazine on the subject of UFOs.

JOHN FOSTER FORBES   *The Unchronicled Past* Simpkin Marshall 1938
Ages Not So Dark The Council for Prehistoric Research in Great Britain 1939
Giants of Britain Thomas's Publications 1945
All three books about psychometry applied to archaeological research.

DION FORTUNE   *Avalon of the Heart* Aquarian Press 1971. An evocation of the magic of Glastonbury.

J. G. FRAZER   *The Golden Bough* abridged edition 1922, now available as a Macmillan Papermac. A study in magic, religion and folklore.

E. O. GORDON   *Prehistoric London : Its Mounds and Circles* Covenant Publishing Co. Ltd, 4th edn 1946

L. V. GRINSELL   *The Ancient Burial Mounds of England* Methuen 1936

PETER HARBISON   *Guide to the National Monuments of Ireland* Gill & Macmillan 1970

JOHN HARRIES   *The Ghost-Hunter's Road Book* Frederick Muller 1968. A gazetteer of ghosts in England, Wales and Scotland.

G. S. HAWKINS   *Stonehenge Decoded* Souvenir Press 1966, and Fontana paperback

F. W. HOLIDAY   *The Great Orm of Loch Ness* Faber 1968. An authoritative account of research into the Loch Ness monster.

ROBERT CHARLES HOPE   *The Legendary Lore of the Holy Wells of England* Elliot Stock 1893

The Journal of Paraphysics   edited by B. Herbert, M.Sc., B.A. (Oxon). (The Paraphysical Laboratory, Downton, Wiltshire)

T. C. LETHBRIDGE   *Gogmagog : The Buried Gods* Routledge & Kegan Paul
The Legend of the Sons of God Routledge & Kegan Paul 1972

The Ley Hunter   edited by Paul Screeton (5 Egton Drive, Seaton Carew, Hartlepool, Co. Durham, TS25 2AT), the only magazine where researchers into leys and allied subjects can exchange ideas and results.

K. E. MALTWOOD   *A Guide to Glastonbury's Temple of the Stars* James Clarke 1964

MORRIS MARPLES   *White Horses and Other Hill Figures* Country Life 1949

H. J. MASSINGHAM   *Downland Man* Jonathan Cape 1926. A fresh look at the meaning of Britain's ancient earthworks.

W. H. MATTHEWS   *Mazes and Labyrinths* Longmans 1922, and Dover Publications paperback 1970

JOHN MICHELL   *The Flying Saucer Vision* Sidgwick & Jackson 1967. The significance of the eternal UFO.
The View Over Atlantis Garnstone Press 1969; revised edition 1972. Leys, serpent power, gematria, and sacred engineering.
City of Revelation Garnstone Press 1972. The numerical constitution and other aspects of the cosmic canon are examined from the evidence provided in sacred writing and the architecture of temples.

ERIC NEWBY AND DIANA PETRY	*Wonders of Britain* Hodder and Stoughton 1968
	Wonders of Ireland Hodder and Stoughton Gazetteers of selected curiosities.
RESEARCH INTO LOST KNOWLEDGE ORGANIZATION	*Glastonbury, A Study in Patterns* 1969
	Britain, A Study in Patterns 1970
NICHOLAS THOMAS	*A Guide to Prehistoric England* Batsford 1960
A. THOM	*Megalithic Sites in Britain* Oxford University Press 1967
	Lunar Observatories Oxford University Press 1971
BRINSLEY LE POER TRENCH	*Men Among Mankind* Neville Spearman 1962. A new picture of mankind's history during the last 10,000 years.
	The Sky People Tandem paperback 1971. UFOs and ancient civilizations.
GUY UNDERWOOD	*The Pattern of the Past* Pitman 1970
JACQUES VALLEE	*Passport to Magonia* Neville Spearman 1970. Is there a link between fairy lore and UFOs?
ALFRED WATKINS	*The Old Straight Track* Garnstone Press 1970. The most important single source book for the student of leys in the British Isles, lavishly illustrated.
S. G. WILDMAN	*The Black Horsemen : English Inns and King Arthur* Garnstone Press 1971
ERIC S. WOOD	*Field Guide to Archaeology in Britain* Collins 1968

Index

Figures in **bold** indicate pages where
the subject is illustrated

283